REVELATION
End Time Guidance

Evangelist
DEA WARFORD

Revelation: End Times Guidance

Copyright 2024

Evangelist Dea Warford

Warford Ministries

www.deawarford.org

All rights reserved. No part of this publication may be reproduced, distributed, or transmitted in any form or by any means, including photocopying, recording, or other electronic or mechanical methods, without the prior permission of the author, except in the case of brief quotations embodied in critical reviews and certain other non-commercial uses permitted by copyright law.

Edited by Linda Stephens

Cover by KDP Amazon

Formatting by ChristianEditingandDesign.com

Published by Warford Ministries

ISBN: 978-1-7352994-3-3

Unless otherwise identified, scripture quotations are from the New King James Version®. Copyright © 1982 by Thomas Nelson. Used by permission. All rights reserved.

Scripture quotations marked as KJV are taken from THE HOLY BIBLE, King James Version. Public domain.

Scripture quotations marked as NIV are taken from THE HOLY BIBLE, NEW INTERNATIONAL VERSION®, NIV® Copyright © 1973, 1978, 1984, 2011 by Biblica, Inc.® Used by permission. All rights reserved worldwide.

Scripture quotations marked GNT are taken from Good News Translation® (Today's English Version, Second Edition) Copyright © 1992 American Bible Society. All rights reserved.

Scripture quotations marked GW are taken from GOD'S WORD®, © 1995 God's Word to the Nations. Used by permission of God's Word Mission Society.

Scripture quotations marked NLT are taken from the Holy Bible, New Living Translation, copyright 1996, 2004, 2015 by Tyndale House Foundation. Used by permission of Tyndale House Publishers, Inc., Carol Stream, Illinois 60188. All rights reserved.

Scripture quotations marked DBY are from THE HOLY BIBLE, Darby Translation. Public domain.

Scripture quotations marked MSG are taken from THE MESSAGE, copyright © 1993, 2002, 2018 by Eugene H. Peterson. Used by permission of NavPress. All rights reserved.

Contents

Preface		5
Introduction		7
Chapter 1.	How to Be Blessed!	21
Chapter 2.	Letters to Churches	29
Chapter 3.	Letters to More Churches	39
Chapter 4.	In the Throne Room	49
Chapter 5.	A Time of Weeping	53
Chapter 6.	The Opening of the Seals	57
Chapter 7.	Come Out	67
Chapter 8.	Angelic Trumpets	71
Chapter 9.	5th and 6th Angels	77
Chapter 10.	The Mystery Revealed	83
Chapter 11.	Finish Your Testimony	87
Chapter 12.	Hell Breaks Loose!	91
Chapter 13.	42 Difficult Months	95
Chapter 14.	The 144,000	103
Chapter 15.	The Victory	111
Chapter 16.	A Done Deal	115
Chapter 17.	Who Is the Harlot?	119
Chapter 18.	Babylon the Great	125
Chapter 19.	The Bride of Christ	131
Chapter 20.	Satan Bound	137
Chapter 21.	The New Earth	157
Chapter 22.	All Curses Gone!	161

Preface

"The Revelation of Jesus Christ, which God
gave Him to show His servants things which
must shortly take place" (Revelation 1:1).

Jesus wants to "show His servants things." To be shown something is "guidance."

I have read through the Book of Revelation every month for years. (I still do today!). Eventually, I began to read it primarily as a devotional and inspirational book. I didn't plan it that way, but the Holy Spirit birthed that in me. I began to look to Revelation for guidance. I wanted its truths to impact my daily life, not just tell me about future events. I wanted to know what the Lord says to Dea Warford through specific verses.

I know most of Revelation speaks of things that haven't yet taken place. But 1:1 says they will "shortly take place." That means they will quickly be concluded once they begin. We will view a lot of future events in my book. And they could be further in the future than you or I expect. Until then, we are told: "**All Scripture is given by inspiration of God, and is profitable for doctrine, for reproof, for correction, for instruction in righteousness, that the man of God may be complete, thoroughly equipped for every good work.**"

"All Scripture" includes the book of Revelation, doesn't it? You, therefore, cannot be "complete" or "equipped" without the "instruction in righteousness." (Those three words are an excellent definition of guidance!) that John's writings can provide. "Instruct" yourself!

Receive guidance for "righteousness" (the right way you should go!) by studying Revelation, not just for end-time events (though we will explore those together), but for what you should do, maybe even today!

"When He, the Spirit of truth, has come, He will guide you into all truth…and He will tell you things to come."

Let the Holy Spirit "guide you into all truth" (your own truth!) for each day, even while He tells us more in Revelation about "things to come."

"**Declaring the end from the beginning, and from ancient times the things that are not yet done, saying, My counsel shall stand, and I will do all my pleasure**" (Isa. 46:10 DBY). Revelation tells us much about "the end." It will happen just as it describes. In fact, it was all determined "**from the beginning.**" But take careful note of this: "**My counsel shall stand.**"

Rick Joyner says, *"God's end time people will "end time."*

Your end-time destiny concludes in the final chapter of Revelation, and your ability to "**stand**" can only be fulfilled if you follow His counsel.

With the help of this book, as perhaps you never have before,

Read Revelation for End Times Guidance

Introduction

My Need for Guidance

"His wife (Jesus' church) made herself ready" (19:7).

It was 1976. I was pastoring a church in Lakeview, Oregon. I had believed all my Christian life in a pretribulation rapture, but I noticed how leaders in the body of Christ had been writing or speaking about the church being here for at least part of the Great Tribulation. I was confused and troubled by it.

I decided to read the book of Revelation all the way through with an open and teachable spirit. That year, I believe the Lord gave me (through the last book in the Bible) GUIDANCE. He showed me two things that would set the course for my future. I was given two pieces of the puzzle of my life. I concluded…

1. The church will go through at least part of the Great Tribulation. I had expected to escape all the terrible events you read about in John's writings. But instead, I had to consider the possibility that I, too, may be one of the reluctant tribulation participants! I was not ready to suffer. I was not prepared for persecution. I did not like the idea at all!

2. God had called me, especially for the last-day reaping of lost souls. The healing mantle for which I had fasted, prayed, and earnestly sought since I was a young man will fall on my shoulders during that time. God's miracle power in remarkable healings will get the world's attention and convince them God is real and to repent and prepare for His coming.

I even "knew" the primary purpose of my life was for that hour and would be fulfilled in a short season. As I aged, I developed greater maturity (and less selfishness!) and an understanding that I was also to train, impart, and release others to do the same. Thus, I have written four books.

Over the following decades, I studied the subject of Christ's coming and began to prepare myself and others for possibly difficult days ahead: physically, emotionally, financially, and spiritually. I also learned from many others.

The late Pastor Jack Hayford was the founding pastor of the Church on the Way, Van Nuys, California. He wrote over 50 books and hundreds of songs. He was considered a leading scholar respected by both charismatic and evangelical churches. He was the number one influencer of my life! I was at Jack's home, and we were discussing Bible prophecy. He told me, and I quote verbatim:

"There is no pretribulation rapture!"

Now, that is the voice of but one respected Bible scholar. You could probably quote others who would say the opposite: "There is a pretribulation rapture." It cannot be both! Either there is or is not a pretribulation rapture. Because both viewpoints have significant ramifications, we need to be prepared regardless of which is correct.

When there are godly, well-studied, proven men of God with polarizing viewpoints, we must humbly seek God for what He wants us to do.

If those who teach a pretribulation rapture are correct, there are only two things you must do:

> 1. Be ready for the Lord to come at any moment and to give an account of your life.

> 2. Do your best to help others come to the Lord before it is too late.

However, if Jack Hayford was correct in saying, "There is no pretribulation rapture," that could mean many things to you and your family, with possibly serious consequences for which you should prepare.

So, with an open mind, explore why men like Jack Hayford and I do not believe we will be raptured out of here before the Great Tribulation begins. This is just my opinion (as everything I write is my opinion). Believe me, I understand that if other godly men say, "The Lord revealed to me the pretribulation rapture is true," that means I must humbly consider maybe I didn't hear from the Lord after all.

Yet, I have not reached my conclusions without what I consider good reasons. If you feel the Lord has shown you that you will never see the Great Tribulation, who am I to say you are wrong? (To be honest, I hope you are right!). But you will now, at least, understand where I am coming from.

It could be a hair-raising roller coaster ride, so fasten your seatbelt.

"For then there will be great tribulation, such as has not been since the beginning of the world until this time, no, nor ever shall be" (Matt. 24:21).

Come Up Where?

"Write the things which you have seen, and things which are, and the things which will take place after this" (Revelation 1:19)

Many who believe in a pretribulation rapture begin their whole ideology with this verse. When Jesus said, "the things that are," those who believe in the pretribulation rapture (Let's henceforth refer to them as PTRs for brevity) are convinced John indicated the entire church age addressed in the letters written to each of the seven churches. Whether they were actual historic churches is not essential for their theology. What is vital to the PTRs is the thought that these churches reveal how the church fared through the ensuing two millennia, and these "things that are" (20 centuries of them!) will end after the rapture (4:1) wraps up the church age. In chapters 5-22, we are shown the "things which will take place after this."

Probably the number one "proof text" PTRs use is 4:1: "After these things I looked, and behold, a door standing open in heaven. And the first voice which I heard was like a trumpet speaking with me. saying, 'Come up here, and I will show you things which must take place after this.'"

Jesus says, "Come up here," to John. To PTRs, that symbolizes the rapture. But consider: Jesus could simply be saying to John, "Come up here. I want to show you something." Thus, the phrase "after this" would not speak specifically of one eternal event (that was still millennia away—the rapture) but simply the following truth Jesus wanted to reveal.

That 4:1 couldn't possibly be referring to anything other than the rapture does not make a strong argument for the most critical event in the history of the church!

PTRs embrace the dogma that Christ will come secretly for the church, and then, after a seven-year tribulation period, He will return to the earth for His Second Coming. Tim LaHaye's *Left Behind* fiction series popularized and furthered this theory (I must remind those who read his books that they are only fiction!). The immensely popular Scofield Notes Bible also sought to prove this theory. And some very prominent TV preachers teach the same.

Yet, nowhere does the Bible conclusively say we will be raptured before the Great Tribulation. This conclusion is based on a broad interpretation of many scriptures, several types from the Old Testament, and assumed symbolisms of Jewish feasts.

Some view the PTR as sacrosanct and part of the gospel. It is essential for you to know that neither the early church nor few in the body of Christ through the ages taught this. In fact, it wasn't even popularly believed until the 1800s when it was taught and promoted by a man named James Darby.

Though many godly leaders today are convinced of its verity, many other godly leaders are just as convinced the church will see at least part of the Great Tribulation

After I saw this in Revelation, for two weeks, I was deeply depressed. Why? Because I was like the people who, at that time, had bumper stickers on their cars that said:

"Warning! This vehicle will be driverless at the rapture."

I was expecting to be driving along enjoying the view, and one day, I would be raptured out of the trials of life. Unfortunately, at that time, I was a carnal Christian (saved but not very sanctified!), and the thought of facing persecution, famines, wars, and even martyrdom was a consideration for which I was not prepared.

This is one reason I am writing this. Many Christians have an escapist mentality, with no thought of any other possibility. I do not want to be just another cry wolf prophet. I'll be the first to admit the end times certainly could be far ahead. Over 50 years ago, I told my backslidden cousin, Dave Williams, that I believed the Lord was returning within a year! Nevertheless, to be forewarned is to be forearmed.

"Be prepared" is a Boy Scout adage. It is always wise to be prepared for the Lord's coming, economic downturns, bad weather, crime, persecution, etc. And I am sure you would agree a Great Tribulation would require great preparation! Here is my advice…

Be ready for Christ to come tonight!

Be ready for the Antichrist to come tomorrow!

An interpretation of Old Testament types (symbolic, metaphorical shadows and pictures pointing to something in the future) is used as "proof" by PTRs. However, some of the types used are a stretch. For instance...Enoch translated without dying before the flood is seen as a type of the church raptured before the tribulation. However, Enoch was only one man; nowhere else in scripture is one man used as a type for the church!

Noah and his family riding safely on the ark while the world was judged with water is another suggested type of the church safe in heaven while the world below is in tribulation. However, Noah's family was still very much here on earth (just riding on water) and were in a smelly ark full of dirty animals for a year. Feeding and cleaning up their messy cages doesn't sound like raptured saints enjoying heaven. Yet, to me, it sure sounds like it could picture the church living safely on an "ark," protected and fed, as the world around them is judged.

Lot and his family, taken out of Sodom and Gomorrah before God destroyed them, are used as a type of the church "leaving" before the tribulation. However, having your wife turned to salt on the way out, ending up living in a cave, and getting drunk with your daughters "raping," you are hardly my idea of a bridal ceremony and the Marriage Supper of the Lamb!

PTRs also claim interpretations of Old Testament Jewish feasts as proof. In one view, the feast of trumpets symbolizes the church's rapture; the feast of atonement is the Second coming (at the end of the tribulation), and the feast of tabernacles is when Christ sets up His Kingdom in Jerusalem.

This interpretation of the feasts could be correct; however, there is no scriptural evidence to prove it. I remind you that Old Testament scholars and even followers of Christ did not understand from the types and feasts that He was the Messiah.

No one knew the feast of Pentecost would be fulfilled by speaking in tongues and a glorious outpouring of the Holy Spirit. It was only after the events were fulfilled that the prophetic purpose of the feast was seen.

None of the disciples knew the candle in the Holy Place represented Christ. No Jew celebrating the Passover understood that Christ's shed blood was symbolized in the Paschal Lamb's blood. No one knew such things until after Jesus' Blood was shed.

Historically, you simply cannot insist on a doctrinal interpretation from a type or symbolic feast until after the type is fulfilled!

"**Now we see through a glass darkly, but then face to face. Now we know in part, but then we shall know even as we are known**" (1 Cor. 13:12 KJV)...is a truth that will stand until Christ finally comes.

And concerning Jewish feasts, there are those who see just the opposite in the Jewish feasts: a post-tribulation rapture.

The Restrainer

A most crucial verse used to "prove" the PTR theory is 2 Thess. 2:6-8: "**And now you know what is restraining, that he may be revealed in his own time. For the mystery of lawlessness** ("lawlessness: Greek--anomia=without law) **is already at work; only He who now restrains** *will do so* **until He is taken out of the way. And then the lawless one will be revealed, whom the Lord will consume with the breath of His mouth and destroy with the brightness of His coming.**"

These three verses continue Paul's 2 Thess. 2:3-5 discussion of the "**man of sin**" (the Antichrist). The "**mystery of lawlessness**" is a mysterious invisible force "**already at work.**" John also refers to this mysterious force of satanically inspired iniquity on earth in 1 John 4:3:

"**And every spirit that confesseth not that Jesus Christ comes in the flesh is not of God: and this is that spirit of antichrist, whereof** ye have heard that it should come; and even now already is it in the world" (KJV).

PTRs believe the Holy Spirit and His influence on earth through His church is what is restraining this "**against Christ**" evil from completely taking over the world at the eventual rise of the Antichrist himself. 1 Thess. 2:7 says, "**He who now restrains.**" He is capitalized by some translators who believe this refers to the Holy Spirit. However, there is no justification in Greek for this assumption! It could just as easily be interpreted as "he" — some man.

PTRs MUST believe this refers to the Holy Spirit, and at the rapture, "**He (the Holy Spirit) is taken out of the way (that is, off planet earth).**" They believe the Antichrist can then come to power with the church and the Holy Spirit gone.

That "**He**" refers to the Holy Spirit is pure conjecture. He could be referring to the Roman emperor who personifies civil government. Throughout history, good leaders in civil governments have restrained "**lawlessness.**" Though Rome was not the church's pal, it tightly controlled crime and rebellions.

Couldn't a financial collapse, worldwide geophysical catastrophe or some world war-related anarchy also end the effectiveness of civil government in holding back the tide of complete lawlessness? Also, couldn't such a scenario be the perfect environment for a great world leader (the Antichrist) to rise to power only to crush the church's influence against lawlessness?

Furthermore, a world without the Holy Spirit's influence cannot be proven scripturally. In fact, He is omnipresent, even in hell: "If I should go down to hell, thou art present" (Psalm 139:8 KJV).

Paul tells us about the rise of the Antichrist in the context of Christ's return in 2 Thess. 2:1-3: "**Now, brethren, concerning the coming of our Lord Jesus Christ and our gathering together to Him, we ask you, not to be soon shaken in mind or troubled, either** by spirit or by word or by letter, as if from us, as though the day of Christ had come. Let no one deceive you by any means; for *that Day will not come* unless the falling away comes first, and the man of sin is revealed, the son of perdition."

Notice: "**The coming of our Lord Jesus and our gathering together to Him.**" Doesn't that sound like the rapture? Doesn't that sound like the time when we rise to meet the Lord in the air? Paul wrote what must happen before that time comes in 2 Thess. 2:3: "**That day WILL NOT COME unless the falling away comes first, and the man of sin is revealed.**" The man of sin is the Antichrist. Paul also said that Jesus would not come until the Antichrist was revealed. So, how could there be a rapture before the time of the Antichrist?

The only way PTRs get around this is to claim this is not referring to the rapture but instead to the Second Coming when Christ will return to earth with His saints. There is no explicit scriptural evidence to prove this.

The "Day of the Lord" could last seven years. There could be a mid-tribulation rapture, a three-and-a-half-year period in heaven (while God's wrath is poured out on earth), and then Christ's and our return to earth. But it seems to me we will be here during the rise of the Antichrist and for at least some of the Great Tribulation!

Do not be lulled into some false hope about avoiding persecution and calamities in the last days (I hope we both do!). But, if you don't escape as soon as you had expected, trust the Lord to help you to "**prepare an ark for the saving of your household**" (Heb. 11:7). Have hope you can ride out any judgments on earth, protected and fed like Noah and His family on the ark!

Concerning any and every prophetic doctrine, always keep in mind Christ's warning (And this was spoken to the Apostles, godly men, who followed Christ closely!):

"See that no one mislead you" (Matthew 24:4 DBY)

The Seven Trumpets

Of all the clues available in John's writings, none throws more light on this subject than the description of seven trumpets that will sound in the closing days of time.

But first, we need to look at 1 Thessalonians 4:15-17:

"For this we say to you by the word of the Lord, that we who are alive and remain until the coming of the Lord will by no means precede those who are asleep. For the Lord Himself will descend from heaven with a shout, with the voice of an archangel, and with the trumpet (note that word "trumpet" which is the focus of our study today) of God. And the dead in Christ will rise first. Then we who are alive and remain shall be caught up together with them in the clouds to meet the Lord in the air. And thus we shall always be with the Lord."

We can agree this speaks of the rapture. But "rightly dividing the Word," we must compare this with other biblical truths.

Revelation chapters 8-11 show the things happening on earth at the sound of seven different trumpets. Here is a quick look at the things these angelic trumpet blasts will release on earth:

> Trumpet 1: "a third of the trees were burned up, and all green grass was burned up" (8:7).

> Trumpet 2: "a third of the sea became blood; and a third of the living creatures in the sea died, and a third of the ships were destroyed" (8:8, 9).

> Trumpet 3: "a third of the waters became wormwood; and many men died from the water, because it was made bitter" (8:10, 11).

Trumpet 4: "a third of the sun was struck, a third of the moon, and a third of the stars…and a third of the day did not shine" (8:12).

Trumpet 5: "he opened the bottomless pit…locusts came upon the earth…to torment them for five months" (9:2, 3, 5).

Trumpet 6: "four angels…were released to kill a third of mankind" (9:15).

There is little argument these six trumpets announce judgments on earth that are part of the Great Tribulation. The debate, instead, is whether the rapture is before, during, or after these trumpets are sounded. Consider another teaching from Paul in 1 Cor. 15:51-5:

"I tell you a mystery: We shall not all sleep, but we shall all be changed— in a moment, in the twinkling of an eye, at the last trumpet. For the trumpet will sound, and the dead will be raised incorruptible, and we shall be changed."

We know this is clearly speaking of the rapture of the church when we receive our new eternal bodies, both those who have already died and are in heaven and those of us still alive on earth. Take note of two phrases:

1. "I tell you a mystery" and 2. "at the last trumpet."

There are only seven trumpets mentioned in Revelation. The seventh one is the last, and John says about that trumpet: "in the days of the sounding of the seventh angel, when he is about to sound, the mystery of God would be finished, as He declared to His servant the prophets" (10:7).

Prophets predicted, and Paul wrote about a "mystery" at Christ's coming in 1 Thess. 4:16 (which will be accompanied by a trumpet!). In Rev. 10:7, John says this seventh and "last trumpet" will "finish" the whole "mystery" (now fully understood) of Christ's return.

I repeat, for emphasis, the trumpet announcing Christ's return in 1 Thess. 4:16 is the seventh and very LAST trumpet, which sounds after part of the Great Tribulation.

"Then the seventh angel sounded. And there were loud voices in heaven, saying, 'The kingdom of this world have become the kingdoms of our Christ, and He shall reign forever and ever'" (11:15).

All seven trumpets appear to be blown during the Great Tribulation. This is a time of judgment, but it is before the bowls of God's wrath are poured out in chapters 15 and 17.

1 Peter 4:17: "For the time has come for judgment to begin at the house of God; and if it begins with us first, what will be the end of those who do not obey the gospel of God?" It is entirely consistent scripturally and historically for God's people to be on earth during evil times (i.e., Israel in Egyptian bondage, Christians and Jews in Nazi Germany, believers killed by the millions in Mao's China and Stalin's Russia).

Paul wrote in 1 Thess. 5:1-9: "the day of the Lord so comes as a thief in the night… But you, brethren, are not in darkness, so that this Day should overtake you as a thief….You are all sons of light and sons of the day. We are not of the night nor of darkness…For God did not appoint us to wrath, but to obtain salvation through our Lord Jesus Christ."

To me, it is clear: the "Day of the Lord" is the period of time when the rule of both man and Satan is terminated on earth, and the Saints receive the Kingdom. The "day of the Lord" is not the 24-hour period of the rapture. Nor is it a 24-hour day of a Second Coming. It does not have to be 24-hours at all: "a day is with the Lord as a thousand years" (2 Peter 3:8).

Considering all the above, can you see the importance of not limiting the rapture to Revelation 4:1 or other debatable texts?

Whatever we may be facing, there is some good news: "…seven

angels having seven last plagues for in them the wrath of God is complete." (15:1).

Since we are **"not appointed to wrath,"** I agree with those who believe God will not treat His church with a dose of "wrath." Yet, I think, we still could "see" part of that wrath being poured out on the world before the rapture.

The marriage supper of the Lamb is a big, thrilling scene expected to occur after the rapture. Yet, it isn't until well after the wrath is poured out, the Harlot of chapter 17 is revealed, and Babylon the Great is fallen in chapter 18, that an invitation is given: **"the marriage of the Lamb has come and His wife has made herself ready…Blessed are those who are called to the marriage supper of the Lamb"** (19:7).

This is undoubtedly further evidence that John goes forward and backward again and again in his prophetic writing. Still not convinced when Jesus is coming? Confused? No, there is no need to be confused. It is just still a mystery!

So, I have shown you why I believe the way I do and am pretty convinced … *There is no pretribulation rapture!*

Yet, I know that is just my humble opinion. Perry Stone, Jonathan Cahn, and John Hagee (wiser men of God than I) have theirs. None of us know about all these things with absolute certainty …**"Watch and pray; for you do not know when the time is"** (Mark 13:33).

The bottom line is…Wisely prepare for His coming, whenever that may be.

"His wife (Jesus' church) made herself ready" (19:7).

Make Yourself Ready with the End Times Guidance you'll discover studying Revelation!

Chapter 1

How to Be Blessed!

"Blessed is He who reads, and they who hear the words of this prophecy, and those who keep those things which are written in it" (1:3).

For years, I let that phrase (**"Blessed is he who reads"**) stand alone, thinking (and teaching)*: "We all will be blessed"* (happy, prosperous, and filled with blessings) *if we but read the book."* Then, I discovered a truth I had missed. There isn't an "or" preceding the following phrase. Instead, there is an 'AND!' So, clearly, that means it is not enough to read Revelation to be blessed. (Lots of people burning in hell today read it. Are they blessed?). John said we would be blessed if we read "...and HEAR..." You know how to read. But what does it mean by "hear?"

I listen to the book of Revelation each month with my Bible app. I always thought by doing this, I was fulfilling what "hear" means. John's vision includes Jesus saying several times in chapters one and two, **"He who has an ear to hear, let him hear."** Was He saying, "*...to all you lucky ones who aren't deaf?"* No, of course not. He spoke to all those who take what is being said seriously and genuinely want to know what God is saying to them personally.

The Book of Revelation is a book about Jesus. And only Jesus used the phrase, 'He who has an ear to hear, let him hear." Why would only our Lord use that phrase? Could it be because, as He said in John 10:27, "My sheep hear My voice?"

We are either sheep or goats, depending on whether we are listening for Him to speak. He is revealed in Revelation as the "**Lord of Lords and King of Kings**" (17:14). He is not just our Savior. He is our Lord and our King. Kings speak orders!

My wife can hear the Lord speak things to her while she is watching a movie! Maybe He speaks to you all the time, too. But, if you are anything like me, you may have to rise early many mornings to spend time alone with Him.

In His presence, whether listening to worship music, praising Him, reading the Word, or just closing your eyes and quieting your spirit to see if He will whisper anything, you are hearing. You are hearing because you are listening! It takes a willing heart to listen for Him to speak. Some fear the Lord might say something they don't want to hear. That is childish and foolish. The Psalmist said in Psalms 85:8 (KJV), "**I will hear what God the Lord will speak: for he will speak peace unto his people, and to his saints: but let them not turn again to folly.**" If you are walking in "folly," you WANT the Lord to tell you so you can repent. If you endeavor to walk righteously, He will say something to bring peace to your heart.

Maybe you learned to listen to the Lord long ago, but now, add to that discipline the "listening" to what Jesus, "the Word of God," says about you in Revelation, giving you guidance for your life. Revelation speaks of bad things that will happen to those who do not have hearing ears. But it also speaks of good to those who do.

Rev. 1:3 guides us on the pathway of blessing…

1. **READ Revelation!**

2. **LISTEN to what the Lord is saying to you.** To be REALLY blessed, reading or hearing is still not enough! One more thing is added to the mix…

3. **KEEP** (other translations say "obey") "**…and keep those things which are written in it.**"

That word "keep" is the key to understanding what Revelation is all about. The MacBook dictionary defines for us (with my comments in parenthesis) …

Keep =

- *Continue doing or do repeatedly or habitually:* (Reading the Word, praying, witnessing, going to church: these things Christ's servants "habitually" do!)

- *Retain one's place in or on…the ground, etc.:* (In James 4:7, we are warned against "**giving place to the devil.**" Stand your ground as Paul warned in Col. 1:23: "**continue in the faith, grounded and steadfast, and not be moved away from the hope…**")

- *Against opposition or difficulty:* (Jesus said in Matt. 7:13, 14, "**Broad is the way that leads to destruction, and there are many who go in by it. Because narrow is the gate and difficult is the way which leads to life, and there are few who find it.**" Are you standing against the opposition and difficulty of serving Christ?)

- *Continue to follow a way, path, or course:* (In Acts 14:22, Paul exhorted disciples to "**continue in the faith,**" saying, 'We must through many tribulations enter the kingdom of God."

Tribulations are a part of the Christian life. Some may even go through the Great Tribulation. You might be going through your private tribulation as you read this today! Whichever, to be saved and enter the Kingdom, you must "**continue in the faith.**")

- *Guard, honor, or fulfill a commitment;* (If you have made a commitment to Christ, you must guard that until you fulfill all being a Christian entails.)

- *Observe…in the prescribed manner;* (Revelation tells of many of those "prescribed manners" as this book will explain.)

A Christian does not just believe things. He does things. "**Be doers of the Word and not hearers only, deceiving yourselves**" (James 1:22). So, to fail to "keep" things we read means we are deceived! Are you deceived unwittingly? To "test" that, determine if you are obeying what Revelation says!

Every generation is intended to receive personal guidance from their Lord regarding the things they are to do. And that includes far more than just refusing the mark of the Beast. If you haven't been, start reading Revelation more than just once a year! As I said, I read it every month. I also mark verses that speak to my heart for that day in yellow (the Bible app allows you to do this. If you prefer reading in a paper Bible, colored pencils do the same).

Then I can pray about that verse and ask God to help it motivate me. You can also reread it at other times during the day. Most nights, I read that special verse one more time before bed, along with some of the verses I have marked from other biblical books (and I may even meditate on it when I wake in the night if I can still remember it!).

If I die tomorrow, the future events depicted in Revelation have helped set the pace for my life and filled me with hope, transforming power, and comforting guidance. Why? Because I read, listen, and earnestly endeavor to "KEEP" the words of Revelation. I am blessed! Are you? *Blessed = "enjoying happiness, bringing pleasure, contentment, or good fortune."* (Merriam-Webster online dictionary). I encourage you to claim the following...

"I am blessed NOW and in whatever the future holds because I will not only read and hear, but I will also obey the book of REVELATION as it guides my way."

In the Spirit

"I was in the Spirit on the Lord's Day" (1:10).

The writer of Revelation, the Apostle John, was condemned to the island of Patmos, where criminals were often exiled. It was a barren, unpleasant island. The Roman Emperor considered Christianity a dangerous cult. Surely, John couldn't cause any harm to the Roman Empire by preaching and gaining converts on Patmos. How ironic it is that a man thought to have effectively been stopped from spreading the Christian "cult" was inspired to write Revelation! That book has been printed, read, preached, and written about for nearly two millennia, converting the lost and strengthening the faithful!

The most critical prophetic document in mankind's history, the book of Revelation, was born because one member of the church made a decision one Sunday (as John wrote in 1:10), "**I was in the Spirit on the Lord's Day.**" Think of "in the Spirit" as the opposite of "in the flesh." It includes things like prayer, worship, the Word, fasting, and seeking to live in the presence of the Lord: "in" those things, as opposed to, say, sports, watching news, movies, comic books, etc. By being 'in the Spirit," like John was that morning, you could make a big difference in your life, family, and church (and in America!). And you don't have to wait until next Sunday!

Are you perhaps desperate for guidance concerning your future? Are present circumstances hinting at an unhappy turn of events? Do you need healing, a deliverance, financial rescue, restoration of a ministry, or other spiritual breakthrough? Be encouraged by John's experience. As John made an effort again to be "in the Spirit, as He did hundreds of times before, something finally and dramatically happened: "**I heard behind me a loud voice, as of a trumpet**" (1:10b).

John suffered much on the isle of Patmos. Likely, there was silence from heaven and no sign of answered prayer. He was an old man, maybe even in his 90s. Many years had passed since Jesus ascended into heaven. But (and only when he was "in the Spirit"), suddenly, John heard "**a loud voice.**" Hallelujah! No more confusion, no more fighting the faith fight, no more feelings of isolation or rejection, no more carefully trying to listen for that "still small voice." A very clear and loud voice sounded. It was an announcement "**as of a trumpet.**"

It was absolutely quiet and then suddenly, there was a loud voice and a trumpet! God is a God of the sudden. Are you discouraged because of a quiet heaven? You need to hear from God this year, this month, THIS WEEK? You long for a loud, clear voice of guidance (like a trumpet) to announce your answer. Everything else you have tried in the past seems to have failed? Then decide this day to do something different from what you perhaps have ever done before. Determine to be "in the Spirit" every Sunday, Monday, Tuesday, Wednesday, Thursday, Friday, and Saturday.

John was near the end of his life, and the most essential details about the end times came at last. As Jesus was with old John, He is ready to reveal to you the most critical details, guiding you to the fulfillment of His destined purpose for your life (revealed by the Spirit).

So, be led by the Spirit as to how you, as a unique individual with a unique walk with your Lord, should do this. But, for sure, let this be your goal, your prayer, and your confession beginning today. Declare it with "a loud voice." Sound your trumpet! Announce to the world, your flesh, and the devil…

"I will be 'in the Spirit' every day!"

Chapter 2

Letters to Churches

"I have a few things against you" (Rev. 2:14).

Chapters two and three contain letters John wrote as Jesus was instructing him. These seven letters were from Jesus Himself, written to "The church at Ephesus," the "church at Smyrna," etc. These were NOT metaphorical churches or prophetic of future churches. These were actual churches located in actual cities. Since two chapters were dedicated to these churches, essential truths must be contained therein. These truths are for Christians, not unbelievers (Though in reading these, sinners can see their need for the Lord, too!).

God commended four of these churches in chapter two, taking note of their good works, but He gave a solid caveat to three of them! For instance, to the Ephesian church, Jesus said in 2:4, **"Nevertheless, I have this against you."** The word against in the Greek means, *"I have (this grave thing) against thee."* (Pulpit Commentary; Eerdman's Publishing Co. 1950). Wow! Those are powerful and sobering words! And, I remind you again that John's words were written to Christians!

Yet today, many preachers continually affirm from a pulpit such things as..."*Jesus loves you. He accepts you just the way you are. Christians are forgiven, not perfect. etc.,"* with little mention of the awfulness of sin, the need for repentance, or the horrors of hell! In one sense, of course, these above statements are factual. But, if these encouraging truths are the only things on the mind of the Lord concerning us, then why would the Bible say that Jesus has anything at all against any Christian if they are forgiven before they even do something wrong (as some preachers put it)?

And why would Jesus say to the church in Pergamus in 2:14:

"I have a few things against you." And to the church in Thyatira in 2:20, **"I have a few things against you?"** Three times, Jesus uses the word against. *"Against" is strong terminology!* There is only one logical conclusion: Being loved, forgiven, and accepted by the Lord does not mean that there aren't some things still in our lives that bring our Lord grave concern. He notices, dislikes (even hates) what hinders our relationship with Him, and our Holy God wants to change these things!

In your time today "in the Spirit," just between you and your Lord, in light of the above truths, ask, *"Lord, is there anything in my life that is displeasing to you, hindering our relationship; that is perhaps short-circuiting my prayers? Because if it is of grave concern to you, I know it should be of grave concern to me!"*

Search your heart today and ask the Lord to help you examine that heart, always keeping in mind the truth that **"The heart is deceitful above all things and desperately wicked. Who can know it?"** (Jer. 17:9). Since Solomon warned, **"He who trusts his own heart is a fool"** (Prov. 28:26), we cannot "know" our own heart or trust our personal appraisal of our lives. We must have the help of the Spirit of the living God to reveal to us those areas Christ is against:

"He who searches the heart knows what the mind of the Spirit is" (Rom. 8:27). Seek the Spirit's help. Pray in the Spirit. Listen to what He is telling you. If you are saved, and you trust Him, and if your heart truly desires to submit to the Lord's will and plan for your life, and you are ready to obey (as we learned in 1:3), He can and will speak to you. Meanwhile, talk to the Lord today and humbly ask Him…

"Is there anything in my life that you are against?"

"To the angel of the church of Ephesus write" (Rev. 2:1).

"Angel" in Greek means "messenger." If by angel, John meant a heavenly angel, this makes chapters two and three challenging to interpret, as it adds a mystical and allegorical sense. In many teachers' minds, a better understanding is that this refers to the church's pastor.

By John's writing, all the other apostles were surely dead. Churches had been organized and led by pastors for some time, as they are even today. There were no TVs, phones, or internet, and many could not read. The Lord's chosen way to communicate was through local pastors, so they, in turn, could communicate what He was saying to the whole church body.

Proof of this concept is that the Lord, throughout the seven letters, commends and rebukes the members of the church. It would be incongruous to think of the Lord rebuking an angel for what was going on in a human's life. The Lord wanted His sheep to know these things. (Angels behind the scenes would already know these things!). The Lord commended the Church in 2:2, 3 (just as Paul did in His Ephesians letter). **"I know your works…you have persevered…and have not become weary…"** But then He added in 2:4 (the 3rd "against" in this chapter):

"I have this against you…that you have left your first love."

I used to preach this means they lost the excitement, joy, and passion they had as new converts. We know newly born-again Christians are highly motivated to win their families to the Lord. So, I wanted to stir up Christians to get excited about their Christianity again. But the Greek profoundly changes this gentle reproof of jaded, long-time followers of Christ. In the verse above, "**...left**" actually means "departed from" and can even refer to "divorce." This is proven to be the meaning contextually because the next verse uses the phrase, "**you have fallen.**" (That is far worse than somewhat backslidden!). Then Jesus gives the added threat that He would, "**remove your lampstand.**"

The lampstand is understood to refer to the lampstand with seven candles in the Holy Place for the Old Testament Tent of Meeting and, later, the Temple. The Holy Place had no windows and was naturally dark, but the priests were to keep the lampstands burning continually. The burning candles giving light in the darkness were a type of Christ, "**the light of the Word**" (Matt. 5:14).

Thus, for Christ to "remove" their "lampstand" would mean the light of His Presence would no longer reside in the church gatherings. This is a far worse judgment than simply removing blessings. What a horrible thought! So, Jesus calls His church to, "**repent**" (2:5). We know there are churches where "the glory has departed." They preach a doctrine of demons. (You don't go to a church like that, do you?) Yet, this word was not just for assemblies of saints. It is also a word to individuals, for He ends the exhortation by saying, "**To him** (That is singular, to the "one" church member!) **who overcomes**" (2:7).

To "overcome" is the repeated phrase to each of the seven churches, as we shall learn. In your devotional time with the Lord, ask yourself and your Lord, *"Have I divorced myself from You? Have I departed from my first love? Am I letting your light shine upon me? Am I one of those overcomers that you promise a heavenly reward?" Do I need to repent?"*

And if you have "divorced" yourself from His church and rarely or never attend church gatherings (except online!), you need to ask the Lord about that too! Hebrews 10:25 says we should, "**not (be) forsaking the assembling of ourselves together, as is the manner of** some..." (I sure don't want the Lord to consider me a "some." I want Him to consider me a "son!") "...**but exhorting one another, and so much the more as you see the Day** (Jesus' coming) **approaching.**" His "Day" is approaching rapidly.

Then, to the church at Smyrna, He says, "**Fear none of those things which you are about to suffer**" (Revelation 2:10). *"Fear not" is the most common phrase in the Bible.* When something bad is happening or about to happen, prophets, angels, and Jesus tell us not to fear. The Lord needed to forewarn them because of what He said would take place: "**Indeed, the devil is about to throw some of you into prison.**"

This verse reveals a lot about our spiritual warfare. Do you think the devil himself appeared to the Smyrna with horns and a pitchfork, took them by the nape of the neck, and tossed them into the closest prison? Of course not. The devil put it in the hearts of leaders in the city of Smyrna to do this. Police or soldiers came to them and arrested them.

"**We wrestle not against flesh and blood**" (Eph. 6:12) does NOT mean humans aren't involved in our battles. It indicates an invisible demon can be behind the problems and persecution men bring to the church or you. This is often the case in marital battles, interpersonal relationships, and church "fights." This imprisonment is done "**that you may be tested.**" The devil wants to test your level of commitment to see if he can get you to turn away from the faith. But the Lord also uses such difficult circumstances to test us to see if we are ready for our greater ministry and to refine us like gold. The Lord wants to ensure our life's value is "gold."

"**When He has tested me, I shall come forth as gold**" (Job 23:10). Fiery trials are one way our works are tested. And God's chosen earthly metaphor for perfection is gold. Rev. 2:10 next adds, "**and you will have tribulation ten days.**" There can be no equivocation concerning this truth: *Christians are called to endure tribulation!*

Paul warned churches in Acts 14:21: "**exhorting them to continue in the faith, and saying 'We must through many tribulations enter the kingdom of God.**" Christians in America know relatively little suffering compared to past generations of believers and many saints today in places like China or some Muslim nations. But get ready! Our time could be coming! None of us relish any suffering or persecution. But take heart! Jesus told the Smyrna church: "**you will have tribulation ten days.**" Ten days is a metaphor for a relatively short season, predetermined by God to end. Any tribulation you are or will be experiencing will soon be over. That's a good place to shout, HALLELUJAH!

Jesus finishes: "**Be faithful until death, and I will give you the crown of life.**" Not all Christians will experience death. Many will be raptured and NEVER taste death. But, until Jesus comes and you receive your "crown of life," your determination must be, no matter how hard things get, that you will be faithful until your final breath! One second after death, it will be worth it all! No believer will be walking around Heaven one million years from now, mumbling, *"Oh, that sure was a terrible ten days back when. My tribulations were awful!"*

Your golden crown of life, resting brilliantly on your head, will forever protect your redeemed mind from such thoughts! "**O Death, where is your sting?**" (1 Cor. 15:55).

"**I know your works, and where you dwell, where Satan's throne is**" (Revelation 2:13). "Satan has a "throne." And it is on earth. Two thousand years ago, it was in Pergamos, which was set on a hill in what is now the modern country of Turkey. It was known for its false religions, cults, and idolatry. Satan is not omnipresent. He can only be in one place at a time. When Revelation was written, he had chosen to center his evil enterprise in Pergamos. I could imagine Satan moved his throne around through the ages; perhaps to Berlin during the time of Nazi Germany? And now, if not some city in the Muslim world, perhaps Los Angeles? Hollywood is the most influential city in the world for evil. It is the epicenter for pornography, movies (which champion homosexuality and blasphemy), worldly music, and so much more. Great place for Satan!

I live in Los Angeles County. People ask me why I would stay here. My answer is that my ministry, children, and grandchildren are here. I assure them I pray and trust the Lord to tell us when, like Lot fleeing from Sodom, to "get out of Dodge." Satan's throne was in Pergamos, yet the Lord did not instruct the church: *"Flee Pergamos! Satan is there! It is so evil. Go to a safer and godlier place."*

Furthermore, v. 13 continues, **"And you hold fast to My name, and did not deny My faith even in the days in which Antipas was My faithful martyr, who was killed among you, where Satan dwells."** Jesus didn't instruct them, *"Run for your lives! You might die a martyr!"* No, instead, he commended them for their faith and faithfulness.

Although there is scriptural justification for fleeing persecution, there are biblical and historical exceptions to that principle. Somebody needed to evangelize that oppressed area of Turkey. Who would win our unsaved neighbors to Christ if we all moved to a Christian community?

I read that Pomona, where I bought a townhome in 2021, then had the highest crime rate in LA County (though that is no longer true today). What person would be better to keep in such a city than an evangelist? Believe and pray the Lord will reveal to you if you need to move from where you live presently (I sure am!). Crime and evil in your city are not sure signs to escape while you can. If you believe you received the Lord's guidance when you moved where you live presently, stay put for now. Only "move with the cloud." Meanwhile, believe this truth:

"The safest place in the Universe is in the will of God."

Jesus then rebukes the Smyrna church: **"You allow that woman Jezebel, who calls herself a prophetess, to teach and beguile My servants to commit sexual immorality and to eat things sacrificed to idols"** (Rev. 2:20). Some feel this woman was an actual false prophetess in the area. Jezebel is at least a metaphor for a very evil woman (You are familiar with her story in the Old Testament). Or she can be a demon of deception. Many leaders in today's church speak of the "Jezebel spirit" out and about wreaking havoc on earth and now even in America!

Rev. 2:18-29 was a letter addressed to the church in Thyatira in what is now known as Turkey. The Son of God first commended them for their **"works, love, service, faith, and patience"** (19). Sounds like a solid church, doesn't it? But then He says, **"Nevertheless I have a few things against you"** (2:20). Oh, oh: there's that word "against!" But He says just **"a few things"** He's against—maybe nothing to be too worried about? But then He explains what those "few things" are: **"you allow that woman to teach and beguile My servants."** He considered the saints in Thyatira **"My servants."** How is it possible Jesus' servants, whom He said had commendable attributes, could be involved in great evil? Jezebel had, in fact, "beguiled" (lured) them to do two things,

> 1. **"commit sexual immorality"** ("fornication"-KJV). Jezebel could still be influencing this pervasive sin of today's church in America because most "Christians" commit fornication or live together before marriage now. It is, unbelievably, accepted as the norm!

> 2. **"and to eat things sacrificed to idols."** Few Americans bow to actual physical idols. Nevertheless, Paul reveals something about this "eating" in 1 Cor. 10:20: **"the things which the Gentiles sacrifice they sacrifice to demons and not to God,**

and I do not want you to have fellowship with demons." Paul had been teaching in this chapter on our communion of the Lord's Supper. He warned about heathen sacrifices or ceremonies, saying that by being involved with such, they were having "fellowship" (communion) with demons! What a thought! Demons! Invited to church services! And demons can be invited (unwittingly usually) into a believer's life!

(In my book *MIRACLES ARE YOUR DESTINY*, I taught a whole section on demonic bondage and shared many of my personal experiences. I also included testimonies of Christians who renounced their deception by demons (some by Jezebel!) and found freedom. You might order it if you haven't already at my website.)

We must be aware of three judgments that will come to Christians "**unless they repent of their deeds**" (2:22).

> 1. "I (Jesus, not the devil!) **will cast her into a sickbed.**" (I have often thought AIDS was a judgment on homosexuality). COVID-19, or the last-day plagues prophesied, could be the fulfillment of this warning.

> 2. "**And I will kill her children with death.**" (Could this not refer to children of God who backslid into fornication and communion with demons and became "children of Jezebel?"). And we know that children always suffer or even die because of their parents' or country's great sins: *Abortion? Hamas atrocities? Last day worship of the Beast?*

> 3. "**and those who commit adultery with her into great tribulation.**" (Greek: tribulation = "suffering," not necessarily the "Great Tribulation").

We must pause here to say Revelation chapters two and three likely had future prophetic significance when revealed to John. As we read these chapters, we cannot avoid the fact that we sadly see a picture of much of the church today in the 21st century. Whether two thousand years ago or tomorrow, God doesn't change or become less Holy. The warnings and judgments we read about still apply. And, as the Lord warned Thyatira, these weren't just "possible happenings" but made clear in 2:23: "**I will**" (do these things!).

What was Thyatira's escape from it all? There was an "unless" added to the mix in 2:22, "**unless they repent of their deeds.**" Thyatira had to repent. The church must repent. You are part of the church, aren't you? Search your heart today! After Jesus' words above…

Do you need to repent?

Chapter 3

Letters to More Churches

"You have a few names even in Sardis who have not defiled their garments" (Revelation 3:4).

Sardis was another church located in what is now modern Turkey. In 3:1, Jesus' words to them were: **"you have a name that you are alive, but you are dead."** He wasn't saying they were dead in trespasses and sins and on their way to hell. Yet, the church was essentially dead (We still use that terminology today to describe a church that seems to have little life in it). We know the whole Sardis church wasn't wholly backslidden because Jesus said in 3:2 that they had some things that remained but added, **"that are ready to die."** The BBE translation says, **"near to death."** The GNT says, **"before it dies completely."**

Apparently, one more deception, one more persecution, one more rebellious sin could put them at the point of no return, but there was still a chance for them if they **"repent"** (3:3). If they didn't, Jesus warned: **"I will come upon you as a thief, and you will not know what hour I will come upon you."** Was this just a coming harsh hand of judgment on Sardis? Or did it speak (metaphorically and prophetically) of Christ's coming? This warning to Sardis is for every church and every Christian in the 21st century!

There is good news in 3:4, **"You have a few names even in Sardis who have not defiled their garments; and they shall walk with Me in white."** The word "few" describes those saved in scripture: **"in the days of Noah, while *the* ark was being prepared, in which a few, that is, eight souls, were saved"** (1 Peter 3:20); **"narrow *is* the gate and difficult *is* the way which leads to life, and there are few who find it"** (Matt. 7:14).

To walk with Jesus in white is the great hope of the church! This promise, however, is only offered to one class of church members: **"He who overcomes shall be clothed in white garments"** (3:5). It says *"He who," not "if you all."* Each individual makes his own choice to be an overcomer. "Overcome" likely means something different to everyone reading this. But it is the only way to be assured we are not dead! What is God calling you to overcome? Does He want you just to be a little better Christian? Or, like Sardis, does it mean that you are in danger of being **"ready to die."**

Repent! Wash your garments in His Blood and make them spotless white! Be at peace because you know your name is *"among a few names."*

"He who has the key of David" (Rev. 3:9). This is Jesus speaking to the church in Philadelphia. Philadelphia was just 30 miles from Sardis (I live 30 miles from Los Angeles!), but He had a very different word for this church. This was the only one of the seven churches He not only had nothing against, but He didn't even have one criticism! Oh, may our home church be like that one! You and me, too!

Jesus described Himself as the one who has a special key: **"the key of David."** This key was mentioned first by Isaiah in 22:22: **"The key of the house of David I will lay on his shoulder; So he shall open, and no one shall shut, And he shall shut, and no one shall open."**

This word was for Eliakim, the finance minister for King Hezekiah, ruler over Judah. As the minister, with this key, Eliakim would have full access to the King's treasuries, though kept behind locked doors. He could shut and lock the door from thieves or unlock it and open the door to access great treasures.

Surely this a type of Christ who would close tightly the door the thief had used to access our potential to enjoy the King of King's riches.

Satan is, "**The thief (who) comes to steal...I have come that they may have life...more abundantly**" (John 10:10). To overcome demonic opposition and to experience this life fully, we need a key He has given to us: "**I will give you the keys of the kingdom of heaven, and whatever you bind on earth, will be bound in heaven, and whatever you loose on earth will be loosed in heaven**" (Matt. 16:19. Jesus Himself gives us these keys. He first inherited them. Then He put them in the church's hands, giving us the privilege of using them to shut doors on Satan and to open kingdom doors.

But there is one caveat in 3:8: "**I have set before you an open door.**" Before we glibly exercise our authority and race through every open door we like, we first must determine if this is a door Jesus has "**set before us.**" The reason we must do this is because when He opens a door for us, "**no one can shut it.**" I have had pastors shut doors on what I thought was God's will for me. Banks, insurance companies, and well-intentioned ministries have also shut doors on me. But, hallelujah, if the Lord opens that door for you or me, *NO ONE CAN SHUT IT!*

That "no one" includes Satan, Washington D.C., or even antichrist powers rising in the world. Jesus gave the Philadelphia church members the above glorious promise because they had fulfilled certain conditions in 2:8:

1. "**you have a little strength.**" What a wonderful truth! We

don't have to be Goliaths in the faith. In God's eyes, if we have stood the test, though it may be just a "little," it is still all the strength we need to open shut doors.

2. "(you) **have kept my word.**" Aren't you doing that to the best of your ability? You are obeying His clear directions and commands. You now qualify!

3. "(you) **have not denied My name.**" Being only 30 miles from Sardis, I am sure many of the same deceptions and persecutions visited Philadelphia. But that church wouldn't budge and stood fast for Jesus!

"His commandments are not burdensome" (1 John 5:3). A relative recently told me it was "hard" to live a Christian life. No! That's a lie: "**My yoke is easy and My burden is light**" (Matt. 11:29).

To abide in Christ, even in the last days, will be easy and not burdensome! (Even with surrounding circumstances notwithstanding!) The Lord will be pleased with us and help us to open or close necessary doors. Assure your heart that you are: *Pressing onward in your 'little strength;" Keeping His Word; Taking your public stand as a Christian.* That isn't too "burdensome" for you, is it?

"I will keep you from the hour of trial which shall come upon the whole world" (Revelation 3:10). Jesus said, "**I will keep you.**" (Keep can also mean "guard"). The above was a specific promise to the Philadelphian church. We know it has not been true of every church throughout the ages. What happened to the church under Hitler, Stalin, and Mao is proof of that. Many prophecy teachers say 3:10 promises that Christians will be raptured before the Great Tribulation. Hopefully, they are right. Regardless of when the Lord comes, we must learn from how Jesus dealt with this one church in contrast to how He dealt with all the previous churches in chapters two and three.

God's promises are conditional. Our responsibility is to fight the good fight of faith to see His promises fulfilled in our lives: **"through faith and patience (we) inherit the promises"** (Heb. 6:12). The Philadelphia church had to do the same. Here were some of the conditions required for them to receive the promise:

1. **"Because you have kept my command to persevere"** (3:10).

2. **"Hold fast what you have"** (3:11). Your salvation, your testimony, and the victory you have gained over sin are things you have! Though faithful up to that point, the Philadelphians still had to be careful to hold on to what they had already gained! And so do you!

3. **"That no one may take your crown"** (3:11). Not Satan, churches, friends, family, or governments; let no one take yours either.

4. **"He who overcomes"** (3:12). This is the requirement for every church and every Christian through the ages.

If we fulfill the conditions, what a glorious list of rewards awaits those who overcome: **"I will make him a pillar in the temple of my God. Never again will they leave it. I will write on them the name of my God and the name of the city of my God, the new Jerusalem, which is coming down out of heaven from my God; and I will also write on them my new name"** (3:12). Now, that is a list that will make it all worthwhile!

All it will take to get all these wonderful rewards is for you to Persevere until the end, hold on to what you already have gained, keep the crown on your head protected from thieves, and Overcome!

Next is the letter to the Laodicean church, and it is eye-opening. 3:20 contains the often-quoted invitation of Jesus, knocking at the door, wanting to come into the life of "any man." I have used that verse thousands of times to encourage people to invite Jesus into their hearts. It was after many years of doing this that I saw for the very first time what the previous verse (19) says: **"be zealous and repent."**

I never made the connection! The mistake I made, as many do, is forgetting chapters and verses were divided by Bible translators with numbers to make it easier to find and quote specific verses. Imagine a pastor saying, *"Somewhere in Revelation, kind of toward the front, there's a verse that says so and so...see if you can find it."* The chapter and verse idea proved to be a great blessing to the church. However, as we read the Word, we often forget this and view a verse with a number before it as separated from the verses before and after. This often results in "taking something out of context."

Before Jesus said He was knocking at the door and wanted to come in, He made a condition, **"be zealous and repent."** Historically, most people who respond to an invitation to accept Jesus into their hearts do not truly repent. It is estimated that up to 10% of those who "pray a sinner's prayer" haven't been born again and don't continue in the faith and get established in a local church. I am sure through the earlier times when I led people in a simple prayer to invite Jesus into their hearts, most of them were stillborn. Then, years back, I started making repentance a significant part of my writing, preaching, and witnessing.

The church in Laodicea (now in modern Turkey) was a center for commerce and banking. Because the city did so well economically, the local church boasted in 3:17: **"I am rich, have become wealthy, and have need of nothing."** That wasn't how the Lord saw them! He warned them they **"do not know that you are wretched, miserable,** poor, blind, and naked." (Again, so much for the cliche, "He accepts you just the way you are.")

It gets worse! "So then because you are lukewarm, and neither cold nor hot, I will spew (Greek: "vomit") you out of My mouth." LUKEWARM CHRISTIANS MAKE JESUS SICK TO HIS STOMACH! Not only were they "lukewarm" toward Him, but Jesus spoke of, "the shame of your nakedness." (A metaphor for how visible their lack of commitment was to the unsaved?). Present-day America is the most shameless example of nakedness (nudity) perhaps in history! Is the partial clothing that even the church has learned to overlook (like on TV) shameful to our Lord? The world can see how much we are like them.

But those individuals who refuse to be among the lukewarm have a glorious promise, "To him who overcomes, I will grant to sit with me on My throne" (3:21).

Imagine the privilege to sit in the throne room of heaven near Jesus! Could you imagine anything greater? To see the way out of lukewarmness and into His throne room may require a revelation: "Anoint your eyes with eye salve that you may see" (3:18). The purpose for which God sent the Apostle Paul to the Gentiles was "to open their eyes, *in order* to turn *them* from darkness to light, and *from* the power of Satan to God, that they may receive forgiveness of sins" (Acts 2:18). People in darkness need their eyes opened. Jesus said, "anoint YOUR eyes with eye salve." So, this is something the person has to do. God, apart from their involvement, doesn't do it for them. It is the choice to turn to God from the darkened path and to apply truth to error.

As with the other churches, there were conditions for the Laodicean church, and for you and me. We must:

1. Anoint our eyes to see

2. Be zealous and repent

3. Overcome!

A Bird Taught Me

It was early one morning in July 2014. I had just read. **"Behold, I stand at the door and knock. If anyone hears my voice and opens the door, I will come in to him and dine with him, and he with Me"** (Revelation 3:20). Minutes later, while still seated in my TV/prayer chair in the living room, I heard a light knock on the screen door. I got up to see what it was. There was my cat, Jewels, tossing up against the door a dead bird she had caught earlier (The bird was still warm, so it had just recently died). It was either a dove or a pigeon. My cat was probably proud of her catch and wanted to show it off or bring it into the house to play with.

My wife, Kathy, has kind of a phobia of birds, so I knew I had to get rid of it before she got up. I took it from the cat, put it in a plastic bag, and went to the big outside trash container to dispose of it. When I came back in and took my place in my prayer chair again, I realized something. I had just read Rev. 3:20. I was suddenly in awe! A dove is a type of the Holy Spirit. That dove (or pigeon; both are in the same bird family) was, in a sense, "knocking at my door." Here is what I knew the Lord was saying to me: *The Holy Spirit wants to come into my life, but I must open the door to Him.* This event proved to be life-changing guidance.

I knew the Holy Spirit was in my life. Jesus was in my heart. But, we're never to settle for that alone. Even the Apostles, who had already been filled with the Holy Spirit on the day of Pentecost (Acts 2:4), were again "filled with the Holy Spirit" in Acts 4:31. The Ephesian church was saved. So, we know Christ was in their hearts. Yet Paul prayed for them, **"that Christ may dwell in your hearts, through faith"** (Ephesians 3:17).

Jesus told His disciples in John 15:7: "If (Yes, it's another one of those conditional promises!) **you abide in Me, and My words abide in you, you will ask what you desire, and it shall be done for you."** Abiding in Christ and having Him abide in us should be our ongoing life pursuit! The Lord was not speaking to me as He would to a sinner, *"Please open the door of your life to me!"* He was saying, *"Dea, I want to reveal myself to you in a much greater way. But you must keep the door open! You must abide with me"* (as husbands share entirely their house with their wives!). Jesus wanted me to learn to share words, to share both our concerns, and to share my destiny with Him right beside me.

There is a beautiful reward for those who truly open the door to Jesus. Not only does He come in to stay, but we get the privilege to "dine with him." The late Jack Hayford was my pastor many years ago. I had the privilege to counsel, talk with him, and even housesit once while he and his wife, Anna, were traveling. But one thing I never got to do was sit down for a meal and "dine with him." Then, the opportunity finally came. Jack invited me and Kathy out to lunch with him after a Sunday AM service. My coveted opportunity had come at last!

Following the service, Jack came to me and said an old friend happened to be unexpectedly visiting that service, and would we mind if he went out for lunch with him instead of us? Of course, we humbly agreed. But another opportunity to "dine" with Jack never came. There is a spiritual lesson in my experience that relates to Rev. 3:20…*A better friend than I was to Jack had the privilege of dining with him.*

We sometimes hear, read, or see someone who seems to have a

much closer relationship with the Lord than we do. They appear to be so in love with Him. They relate precious experiences with Him: deep insights into the Bible, special words, dreams, and even visions. Like with Jack Hayford, somebody who is a better friend earns an opportunity for intimacy with the Lord, intimacy we possibly haven't achieved yet. It isn't that Jesus loves them more, but *could it be that they love Jesus more?*

Nevertheless, there are things we can do to fall more in love with Jesus and to experience greater intimacy with Him. We see several steps mentioned to the Ephesians:

> 1. **"Hear my voice"** (We learned in earlier studies that this means to be listening carefully to what He may be saying)

> 2. **"and opens the door."** (Jesus won't demand or force His way into our lives. We must get out of our easy chair, fearless of any thieves "out there," and give Jesus an open-door invitation to come in.)

> 3. **"to him who overcomes."** (There is that pesky requirement again! There is no other way around it! We must overcome our sins!)

You are saved. The Holy Spirit is in you. But are you dwelling in Christ, and is He dwelling in you?

Is He knocking today?

Is your door wide open?

Are you an overcomer?

Chapter 4

In the Throne Room

"They do not rest day or night, saying: Holy, holy, holy, Lord God Almighty" (4:8).

Before we visit the throne, I must speak parenthetically of something important. To describe prophetic events in other than a sequential method is totally in keeping with the method God used in prophetic words from Old Testament prophets. For example, in Isaiah 60, he describes events in the last days, but in Isaiah 61:1, 2, he speaks of Christ's first coming. Jesus quoted this very verse in Luke 4:18, 19 adding, **"Today this Scripture is fulfilled in your hearing."** In 65:17 Isaiah speaks of the new heavens and new earth (a very future event!), but then in 66:8, he goes backward in time and prophesies Israel's birth as a nation (in the 20th Century!).

This method of prophecy, panning back and forth through time, can be seen in Hollywood productions. Some movies are linear. Each scene shows the ongoing events in the lives of those involved in the plot line. Some have "flashbacks" where characters' lives go back and forth from adulthood to childhood, sometimes frequently. The idea is to help us understand how choices impacted the movie's ending.

Jesus is eternity's greatest showman. Read the angels' reaction to seeing Jesus create the heavens and the Earth: "**Where were you when I laid the foundations of the earth?...When the morning stars sang together, and all the sons of God shouted for joy**" (Job 48:4, 7). No Hollywood filmmaker could ever match Jesus in His ability to make "the greatest show on earth." And the creation will be nothing compared to the grand finale that He's preparing for His closing curtain call on earth.

The Lord can do whatever He chooses. If He chose to give Old Testament prophets bits and pieces from their present dealings with Israel and intermix them with visions of the world's greatest final events, then He certainly could have done the same with John.

That John was simply reporting events as He was shown them makes the best sense because, as we will soon see in this study, we will follow the scriptures back and forth from scenes that picture the rapture to the wrath, to the pre-wrath, back again to the rapture, then to the mid-wrath, etc. You either force things to say what fits your prophetic scheme, whether it makes sense to everybody else or not, or you just have to admit maybe some prophetic things are not as cut and dry as some have concluded.

Now let's take gaze into the Throne Room of heaven: "**They do not rest day or night, saying: Holy, holy, holy, Lord God Almighty**" (4:8).

This verse speaks of something the "four living creatures," who are positioned around the throne, are saying "day and night" (that's like our 24 hours a day!). Notice they don't even take a break from this activity: "**They do not rest.**" Also, note they were not saying, "love, love, love"... or ... "grace, grace, grace." Yet, to hear many of today's preachers, you would think love and grace are the two terms that best describe God. Yes, "God is love," and He is the "God of all grace," yet these are NOT what those closest to Him are celebrating. Let this sink in…

Day and night, without stopping, these beings situated closest to God were seen by John continually declaring His holiness!

Some people think love is the highest attribute of God. It isn't. Holiness is the highest attribute of God. Here's proof: The love of God is NOT enough to save a lost sinner and deliver him from an eternity in hell unless He comes through Christ. Only Jesus' substitutionary death on the Cross sufficiently satisfies the need for a Holy God to overlook man's sins. Today's mantra by many so-called Christians is: *"A loving God would not send a sinner to an eternity in a Lake of Fire."*

Here's the mantra, however, of those closest to this loving God. Their "holy's" are the equivalent of saying *"A Holy God cannot allow an unholy sinner (who blasphemes His Name, and repeatedly speaks unholy f-words, and celebrates nudity, etc.) in His Presence."* One might ask, "But what if they go to church and don't do really bad things? Surely they could make it to Heaven!" It might be a pleasant thought, but here's God's answer to that: **"Without holiness, no one** ("No one!" is NOT very inclusive) **will see the Lord"** (Hebrews 12:14 NIV). Case dismissed!

Isaiah 6:3 tells us the Seraphim angels also cry, **"Holy, holy, holy is the Lord of hosts"** (Hosts in Hebrew means "armies."). These angels add to their proclamation, **"The whole earth is full of His glory!"** We often hear people describe "praying in the spirit" as the language of heaven. But I submit to you that the language of heaven is to cry "holy!"

When the Lord revealed this truth to me, it changed my life. How often since then have I humbly lifted my hands to Heaven and joined the living creatures and the Seraphim to cry out and pray, **"Holy, holy, holy is the Lord of hosts…The whole earth is full of His glory!"** Then I add, *"Lord, let my hands be full of your glory; let my* *mouth be full of your glory; let my eyes be full of your glory, etc.* (continuing with other parts of my body). Then I ask Him to, *"Let my family and Warford Ministries be full of His glory."* What do you want Him to fill with His glory? From Revelation chapter four, we get some clues on how to experience the glory of heaven in our lives on earth.

- Live a holy life!
- Declare His glorious Holiness in your devotions!
- Be clothed in white robes to gain access to the Holy Place!
- Learn to speak the language of Heaven!

Practice now! Declare it...

"Holy, holy, holy."

Chapter 5

A Time of Weeping

"So I wept much, because no one was found worthy to open and read the scroll" (Rev. 5:4).

In 5:1, John had just seen a vision of God seated on His throne. In His right Hand was a scroll. It was written inside and on the back and was sealed with seven seals. An angel asked in 5:2: "**Who is worthy to open the scroll and to loose (break) its seals?**" The answer was given in 5:3: "**And no one in heaven or on the earth or under the earth was able to open the scroll, or to look at it.**"

John's response to this word is very interesting: "So, I wept much, because no one was found worthy to open and read the scroll or to look, at (into) it" (5:4). "But one of the elders said to me, "Do not weep. Behold, the Lion of the tribe of Judah (This is the only place in the Bible where Jesus is called "Lion of the tribe of Judah"!) has prevailed to open the scroll and to loose its seven seals'" (5:5).

In the throne room, John was then shown "a Lamb as though it had been slain" (5:6). We know who this is! "Then He (Jesus) came and took the scroll out of the right hand of Him who sat on the throne" (5:7).

Chapter 5 does not tell us what the seven seals were about, but they will be revealed to John in chapters 6-8.

The most moving part of this chapter, at least to me, is that in 5:4 John **"wept much."** He wasn't just saddened, or a tear came to the corner of his eye. He **"wept much."** The GNT says John **"cried bitterly."**

Why would a sealed scroll be so important to John? I submit for your reflection that John was being shown truths that would affect the church and the whole world! He was old and knew he did not have much more time to minister. If what was written in that scroll would help him give a more complete prophecy of the future, he desperately wanted to see its contents.

After the death of Lazarus, hearing the hopelessness and sorrow of those who lost a loved one and were faced so vividly with the fear of what happens after death, **"Jesus wept"** (John 11:35). John wept too. How often have we wept over sick and dying people? How bitterly have we borne a burden for the lost who face the horrors of hell? Jesus also wept over those facing a terrible future at the hands of invading Roman soldiers: **"But as he came closer to Jerusalem and saw the city ahead, he began to weep"** (Luke 19:41 NLT). Have we wept over our city or nation, especially when prophets are predicting great difficulties ahead of us?

Yet, we can do things other than weep. We can give to missionaries taking the gospel to the lost heathen. We can witness, hand out tracts, and invite people to our church. There is one more action we can take that is revealed in 5:8: **"Now, when He had taken the scroll, the four living creatures and the twenty-four elders fell down before the Lamb, each having a harp, and golden bowls full of incense"** (What is that incense that is such a pleasant odor in the throne room?) **"which are the prayers of the saints."** Your prayers count in heaven, though you might not feel like they do in your prayer closet!

The mention of prayers being laid up in a golden bowl is in the context of the scroll which reveals the seven seals of chapters 6-8. This should encourage us that our prayers to heaven, though not yet answered, in the closing days will prevail at last! Seemingly unanswered long-term intercessions will quickly be fulfilled. Unsaved family members and friends, with the help of your prayers (even if you are not around to see it), will repent, and get ready for the judgment (even if only at the last moment!).

Jesus loved the world so much that He carried a burden for it all the way to the Cross! Share His burden and carry your cross...

Weeping...Witnessing...Giving...Praying!

Chapter 6

The Opening of the Seals

> **"Now…the Lamb opened one (the first) of the seals" (6:1)**

The opening of the seals in chapter 6 describes some of the early events of the end times. These things could be a continuation of the "beginnings of sorrows" Jesus forewarned in Matt. 24:8. The sobering events you are studying will possibly happen to you or at least to many you know and love. First, we are introduced to what has popularly been referred to as: THE FOUR HORSEMEN OF THE APOCALYPSE.

1. THE WHITE HORSE…
"And I looked and behold, a white horse (This could be actual or metaphorical but was understood as the color of a horse led by a general or a king.) **And he who sat on it had a bow; and a crown was given to him, and he went out conquering and to conquer" (6:2).**

This white horseman is a picture of the Antichrist, the false Messiah, imitating or mocking Jesus, who will return riding on a white horse (see 19:11). The Antichrist goes out as a conqueror and will eventually conquer virtually every nation on earth!

Other metaphorical horsemen are enabled to ride through the earth after the Antichrist comes to power. Earth will then be faced with the greatest challenges in its history. You may already be in heaven by then. But, while studying chapter 6, I suggest it would be wise to continually be asking yourself (and the Lord), *"Am I spiritually ready in case I have to live through the times revealed in Revelation 6?"*

2. THE RED HORSE...

"Another horse, fiery red, went out. And it was granted to the one who sat on it to take peace from the earth, and that people should kill one another; and there was given to him a great sword" (6:4).

The relative peace we enjoy today could soon be taken away. "People will kill one another" sounds like not just some local conflict but an international one involving countries, states, cities, and as well as neighborhoods. (Perhaps gang wars, as we read of in Mexico. Or starving Americans, normally good citizens, willing to kill, if necessary, to feed themselves or their families!)

It is the fulfillment of Christ's words in Matt. 24:7: "nation will rise against nation, and kingdom against kingdom."

3. THE BLACK HORSE...

"And I looked, and behold, a black horse, and he who sat on it had a pair of scales in his hand" (6:5). This pictures a time of great scarcity: "And I heard a voice in the midst of the four living creatures saying, 'A quart of wheat for a denarius' and three quarts of barley for a denarius'" (6:6). That was the equivalent of a day's wage at that time. Imagine working all day for a loaf of bread! In Germany, during hyperinflation in the 1920s, a loaf of bread that normally cost 163 marks sold for over a million!

6:6 continues "and do not harm the oil" Scarcity of oil could happen overnight if a major war breaks out in the Middle East. The cost of gas is already double in 2024 from what it was a few years back. A sign of the end times? **"and the wine."** Two thousand years after this writing of John, fine wines still symbolize "the good life." (Sipping drinks in a fine Italian restaurant, for instance). The best wines can only be afforded by the rich. Most of us (I'm included) have had to stop buying certain of our favorite foods because they have just become too expensive! Cokes were a dime when I was a kid. Now they can be $3.00 or more!

This hyperinflation could be one cause of the "famines" foretold by Jesus in Matt. 24:7. Famines will help pave the way eventually for the mark of the beast when starving people will take the mark to "buy and sell." Are you ready to trust the Lord if world war or local uprisings challenge your peace? Can you trust Him in a time of famine? (Or do His promises only work in times of peace and prosperity?)

Your devotional times should always be times to use promises in the Bible to guide you, build your faith, and to encourage yourself in the Lord! Following is a list of end times precious promises: **"In famine He shall redeem you from death, And in war from the power of the sword. You shall laugh at destruction and famine"** (Job 5:20...22; **"Behold, the eye of the Lord is on those who fear Him, On those who hope in His mercy, To deliver their souls from death, and to keep them alive in famine"** (Psalms 33:18, 19); **"They shall not be ashamed in the evil time, And in the days of famine they shall be satisfied"** (Ps. 37:19).

And never forget Psalm 91!

If we see the promises of Revelation being fulfilled right before our eyes, we can also trust all the other promises in the Word to be fulfilled when we need them the most! You may need them! Learn them!

4. THE PALE HORSE...

"I looked: behold, a pale horse. And the name of him who sat on it was Death" (6:8). I once posted on my Facebook page that I was *"somewhat of an expert on death"* (performing funeral services for maybe 300 people and preaching about death and hell for over half a century). Someone commented on my post, *"It's your business what you preach, but I try to be an expert on life."* (hinting I should concentrate more on life than death). Well, an evangelist probably looks at death and the hell thereafter awaiting many with greater awareness and sobriety than the average Christian. (Thus, He led me to write my book *EVANGELIST* to inspire others to win souls and the book *ABOUT THE FUTURE* to describe more about death and hell).

Eccl. 3:11 says, "**He has put eternity in their hearts.**" Eternity is in my heart, and since death is the pathway into eternity, I study it and think about it a lot! It is very important to understand death since, apart from the Lord coming first, we will all experience it one day!

Just as important is what the book of Revelation tells us about the big part death plays in the coming end times: "**When He opened the fourth seal, I heard the voice of the fourth living creature saying, 'Come and see.' So I looked: behold, a pale horse. And the name of him who sat on it was Death, and Hades (ready to take people immediately to hell!) followed with him. And power was given to them over one-fourth of the earth, to kill with the sword**" (Rev. 6:7, 8).

One-fourth of the earth will be affected by the pale horse. Not just by war, but 6:8 adds the pale horse kills with "hunger." One of the primary causes of hunger (or famine), is drought. Growing food requires water. There are three major sources of water coming into the Los Angeles area. (88% of its water is from exterior sources!). Scientists have discovered one 7.9 magnitude earthquake on the San

Andreas fault could damage or destroy all three of our water sources at the same time!

Rick Joyner (among my most respected leaders in the body of Christ) believes millions of Southern Californians will thirst to death because of future catastrophes. With freeway overpasses destroyed and roadways buckled, how long would it be until enough food for over 22 million people could be shipped in, not to mention water?

Currently, *"Sub-Saharan Africa is the region with the highest prevalence (percentage of population) of hunger. One person in four there is undernourished."* (Source: World Food program, wfp.org). "One in four" quoted above is interesting because that is the exact fraction, "one-fourth of the earth," mentioned in 6:8!

The Pale Horse, in addition to killing by war and famine, also kills with "death." Various translations interpret this word as plague, pestilence, or disease.

Then the last tool Death uses to destroy is when he will "**kill by the beasts of the earth**" (6:8). Mankind has always been subject to death from animals, and sometimes as a form of judgment! In 2 Kings 17:25, The Israelites had been taken captive, and Assyrians took possession of Samaria. But "**they did not fear the Lord; therefore the Lord sent lions among them, which killed some of them.**"

We read in the news how pets turn unexpectedly on their owners and kill them. Imagine an end-time scenario where the entire animal kingdom rises against humans. Pet snakes slither through bedrooms to kill their owners. Pet birds spread a new "bird flu" that, in past years, killed hundreds but ultimately kills millions. Could it be because of famine, starving domestic animals, like cats and dogs, suddenly realize the only way they will stay alive is with the help of their "master's" flesh? In addition, many bacterial diseases begin and are spread by animals. Some believe bats spread COVID-19. The AIDS epidemic began in Chimpanzees. The Black Plague is thought to have been spread by rats.

Then, in the New Testament, Matt. 8:30-32 tells the story of two demon-possessed men living in the tombs. When Jesus commanded the demons to come out, they begged Jesus to allow them to enter the bodies of a nearby herd of pigs. Jesus permitted them, and the demons drove the pigs wild until they all ran into the sea and drowned. Demons from hell could be unleashed to enter domesticated animals, driving some to do things they would never usually do, like kill people.

The pale horse will be the ruthless agent of death by the animal kingdom. So, just in case we haven't been raptured yet and are still here when these events take place, we have precious promises to claim as believers. Jesus said, "**I give you power to tread upon serpents and scorpions**" (Luke 10:19), and "**They shall take up serpents**" (Mark 16:18). When a snake attacked Apostle Paul, he "**shook off the creature into the fire and suffered no harm**" (Acts 28:5). Let's plan to do the same!

When driving in areas where deer or other animals may cross the road, I will often claim Job. 5:23, "**And the beasts of the field shall be at peace with you.**" If we are not to "**fear not them which kill the body, but rae not able to kill the soul**" (Matt. 10:28KJV), how much more should we not fear animals! Again, the most common phrase in the Bible is: "Fear not."

And all the biblical "fear nots" remain valid and are not nullified when Revelation six takes place!

The Fifth Seal

"When He opened the fifth seal, I saw under the altar the souls of those who had been slain for the word of God for the testimony which they held" (Revelation 6:9).

Martyrdom best describes the fifth seal! Answer the following question, *"If someone had a gun pointed at my head and asked me, 'Are you a Christian?' What would I say?"* My family members and I were discussing this question. Both my wife and son, Nathan felt it would have been acceptable to answer an executioner with a lie to save their life. Nathan said he would have told the shooter if asked if he was a Christian, "No!" And then he would have just asked the Lord to forgive him later. Would the Lord have forgiven him?

Lying is a great sin: **"All liars shall have their part in the lake which burns with fire and brimstone, which is the second death"** (Rev. 21:8). Yet, can we never lie, even if it would save ours or somebody else's life? If a rapist with a gun knocked on my door and asked, *"Are there any women in the house?"* Do you really think the Lord would expect me to say *"Yes, my wife is in the master bedroom and my daughter is in the other bedroom? If you insist, come on in."* Of course not! And there is a Scripture for this, too: **"Answer a fool according to his folly"** (Prov. 26:5).

Does a rapist deserve an honest answer that would bring great harm or even death to someone? And can we ever lie to escape persecution? Even Peter lied and denied Christ to keep from persecution. The Lord forgave him, and He became one of the most influential leaders in church history. If God forgave Peter for lying about his faith, we have to admit there are fine lines on this subject and few hard and fast rules.

Corrie Ten Boom's *The Hiding Place* tells the story of when the Nazis came to a home where they were hiding Jews in a hidden compartment with a secret door under the kitchen table. As the family members were seated at that table, the Nazis asked if they were hiding any Jews there. A young Christian lady felt she could not lie and said, "Yes." The Nazis asked, "Where?" Compelled by her conscience, fear, or both, she blurted, *"Under the table!"* and then burst into hysterical laughter. Thinking they were being mocked, the Nazi's disgustedly stormed out of the house. The Jews were saved despite a Christian telling the truth. God's grace can overcome any obstacle!

Throughout scripture, God at times supernaturally protects His children from death by persecution. It is wise and proper to seek to avoid any persecution. Jesus told His disciples, **"When they persecute you in this city, flee to another"** (Matt. 10:23). Don't look for persecution! But when it comes, be prepared for how you will respond.

Paul was protected from death by stoning and was more than once scooted off to safety from his persecutors by church members until (tradition says) he was finally beheaded for his faith. Jesus literally walked through his persecutors more than once, but when His time at last came, He submitted himself to them, and they crucified Him. Ultimately, the day may come when there is no question about what you must do when asked, *"Are you a Christian?"*

If we aren't raptured before the rise of the Antichrist, we one day might be given the choice of receiving the mark of the beast or laying down our lives for Christ. We see on the news what I, and many other Christian leaders, have been saying for a long time is already coming to pass, *"Persecution is coming to America!"*

Take careful note of Rev. 21:8. When it mentions the people who find their eternal destiny is the lake of fire, the first group is the *"cowards."* Matthew 10:33 warns: **"Whoever denies Me before men, him I will also deny before My Father who is in heaven."** Denying Christ (By our words, our actions, or our lack of words or actions!) is serious business. Facing persecution requires not being cowardly!

It will keep getting worse and worse, culminating in the Antichrist's worldwide reign. Christian . . . *Will you be one of those who falls away because of the increasing commitment required of Americans who follow Christ? Will you leave your church for fear because of frequent church shootings? Will you lie to save your life? Will you take the mark of the beast?* Think it through. Pray it through. Because one day soon, with eternity at stake, you might be asked at the point of a gun or at the base of a guillotine *"Are you a Christian?"*

The Sixth Seal

"The great day of His wrath has come, and who is able to stand" (Revelation 6:17).

This last seal from chapter 6 further proves that we cannot interpret Revelation sequentially. The opening of the sixth seal unleashes things like, **"the sun became like a sackcloth of hair…and the stars of heaven fell to earth…then the sky receded as a scroll when it is rolled up…and every mountain and island was moved out of its place"** (6:13-14). In response to these universal events, men **"hid themselves in the caves…and said to the mountains and rocks, "Fall on us and hide us from the face of Him who sits on the throne and from the wrath of the Lamb!"** (6:15, 16). I cannot see this as anything other than the Second Coming of Christ! Yet it is in chapter 6, long before the many other things in chapters 7-18 take place, which with little doubt happen before 6:13-14.

Do NOT take for granted that what we read in the following chapters has nothing to do with you (because you will be in heaven). You might be, and I hope I am there with you! But the Lord put all these highly detailed descriptions of earthly events for you to read for a reason. So… **Read them!**

Chapter 7

Come Out

> "These are the ones who came out of
> the great tribulation" (Rev. 7:14).

There is a group of Christians who will **"come out"** of the **"great tribulation."** You CANNOT come OUT of something you aren't already in! That is why I do not believe in Eternal Security. Paul wrote the Galatians in 5:4, **"You have become estranged from Christ, you who attempt to be justified by law, you have fallen from grace."** You cannot "fall" from a place where you aren't already, thus, 7:14 is evidence Christians will still be here, at least for a season, when the tribulation is upon us.

The only argument to contradict this is to assume these are primarily new Jewish converts who get saved during the tribulation, so they weren't raptured. To help defend this theory, some point to the 144,000 of 7:3, 4: **"Do not harm the earth, the sea, or the trees till we have sealed the servants of our God on their foreheads. And I heard the number of those who were sealed, 144,000."**

It is argued that these 144,000 are Jews who are chosen to preach the gospel on earth, since all the true Christians, many believe, were already raptured in 4:1. The problem, however, is that nowhere does the Bible say these 144,000 were chosen to preach. And it is simply not good hermeneutics (The science of biblical interpretation) to assume a verse says anything that cannot be supported by the context or other references. (We will learn more about this 144,000 in chapter 14).

One of the reasons I believe the Lord revealed to me (over four and a half decades ago) that we may experience at least some of the Great Tribulation is because He knew I would have a writing venue whereby I could help prepare (and warn!) Christians (like you?) for these final few years that may be just ahead of us.

If you have believed the pretribulation rapture theory and have held onto that, I am not demanding you give it up (Again: yes, you could be right, and I am wrong). But I am asking you to remain teachable and at least hear from one who has a different perspective.

Has the Lord brought **"us to the kingdom for such a time as this?"** (Esther 4:14). Has He led you to read my teachings to help you be prepared for something for which you might otherwise not have been prepared? If the thought of being one of those Christians here during the Great Tribulation is difficult for you, find comfort from the happy ending for those who "come out" in 7:14-17 KJV:

"These are they which came out of great tribulation, and have washed their robes, and made them white in the blood of the Lamb. Therefore are they before the throne of God, and serve him day and night in his temple: and he that sitteth on the throne shall dwell among them. They shall hunger no more, neither thirst any more; neither shall the sun light on them, nor any heat. For the Lamb which is in the midst of the throne shall feed them, and shall lead them unto living fountains of waters: and God shall wipe away all tears from their eyes."

Every Christian has a happy ending! Whether you die tomorrow, get raptured the next day, or struggle through three and a half years of "Jacob's Trouble," you still win, and win like a champion!

So there! You wondered when you bought this book if it had a happy ending. Well, it does! I promise you…

You Will Have a Happy Ending!

Chapter 8

Angelic Trumpets

"And I saw the seven angels who stand before God, and to them were given seven trumpets" (8:2).

Before we look more closely at the sounding of the trumpets, be encouraged by the promise in 8:3-5 that an angel will take a golden censer of incense and **"Offer it with the prayers of all the saints… filled it with fire from the altar, and threw it to the earth. And there were noises."**

This **"throwing the censer"** to the earth is a time of answered prayers! Sudden answers to "the prayers of all the saints." Prayers previously kept in store in the golden bowl (5:8) but now thrown to the earth will result in miracles galore! **"And there were noises."** Acts 2:1-4 tells us of the birth of the church at Pentecost. **"And suddenly there came a sound from heaven, as of a rushing mighty wind"** (2:2). That would be quite a "noise!" There was a "suddenly" at the birth of the church. It was a quick work then, and another quick work is coming soon! At Pentecost were **"tongues of fire"** (2:3). The angel's censer was **"filled with fire (also)."**

The end of this planet and the coming of Christ will be a climax, outshining every event and everything that has ever been seen throughout history! Is it this year that the church will begin to rise to its kingdom rulership with its Lord, far exceeding the grandeur of its birth? When it does, as at Pentecost, it will include a Suddenly! Fire! And a Noise! We will become a church filled with power, resulting in millions and millions brought into the kingdom!

(Whew, pardon me while I catch my breath!)

And that, my friend, is why, I believe, the Lord might just keep us here on earth a little bit longer instead of being raptured before the world needs us more than ever!

Angelic Climate Change

Angels get terribly busy in chapter 8.

1st Angel sounds:

"The first angel sounded: And hail and fire followed, mingled with blood, and they were thrown to the earth; and a third of the trees were burned up, and all green grass was burned up" (8:7). The phrase "fire and blood" could be symbolic, but since the blood in the judgment of Egypt was real, we can probably expect actual blood!

It says, "and a third of the trees were burned up." Climate Change from automobiles? How about climate change from angels? This is one primary reason why I am NOT a tree-hugging environmentalist! If we are close to the end and the Lord Himself, through an angel, is going to destroy one-third of the trees on earth, should I worry about replanting enough trees for 100 years from now?

(I believe in protecting the environment, of course! I reuse plastic bags and don't litter. I try not to waste water or electricity. When I refill my car with gas, I try to prevent spillage. But it is the extremes, at any cost, that are being pushed on America that I reject!)

The angel's work continues, **"and all green grass was burned up."** This is why I don't mow my grass. Angels are going to do that for me!

Extreme environmentalism—an invention of Satan? Think about it. Some estimate it will take over 90 trillion dollars (Yes, that is a trillion with a "t") to fully implement the "Green New Deal." Satan knows before he can raise up the Antichrist with his mark, he first has to have America out of the way. Why? Because of our mightiest military, nationalism, defense of democracy around the world, and our free economy. What better way to destroy America's economy than by taxing us all into poverty to so-called "Save the Planet!" If America's economy fails, the whole world will follow suit! Satan knows this well, so (I am convinced!) he invented extreme environmentalism. The proponents' cry is…

"Climate change is an existential threat!"

My response to that is…

"Sin is an existential threat!"

2nd Angel Sounds:

"And something like a great mountain burning with fire was thrown into the sea, and a third of the sea became blood; and a third of the living creatures of the sea died, and a third of the ships were destroyed" (8:8, 9). A "great mountain burning with fire" is how one who didn't know modern astronomy would likely describe a gigantic meteor hitting the atmosphere, bursting into flame, and crashing into the sea. One-third of the creatures in the sea will die (So much for the "Save the Whales" campaign!). God isn't as concerned for animals as He is for man. "Is it oxen God is concerned about?" Paul rhetorically wrote in 1 Cor. 9:9.

God commanded Israel to slay thousands of animals in sacrifice to Him. That should say something to us! Even Jesus himself "killed" some fish and roasted them on a fire for the disciples to eat, saying in John 21:12 KJV: **"Come and dine."**

The Lord wants us to enjoy our animals. They are a gift from God to us, as many widows would attest! However, because "we have the mind of Christ," we realize the world is out of balance in its understanding of the things that really count (i.e. Thinking that killing a baby is a woman's reproductive right but saving a dog left in a box along a highway is a most noble deed!). The Tribulation will help get EVERYBODY's attention making them reconsider what really matters in life!

3rd Angel Sounds:

"A great star fell from heaven, burning like a torch, and it fell on a third of the rivers and a third of the waters became wormwood; and many men died from the water" (8:10, 11). Politicians and prophets are warning us that terrorists have plans to poison our water systems. Wormwood is a poisonous plant and, in scripture, is a symbol of bitterness. Water, which man is most dependent on for life, will one day bring death to many!

Jeremiah 2:13 says: **"They have forsaken Me, the fountain of living waters, And hewn themselves cisterns—broken cisterns that can hold no water."** Mankind chose $H2O$ over HIM, and one day they will pay for it! Oh, may men turn to the Lord and drink of the water of life Jesus offers (John 7:37-39) before it is too late).

It is not Hamas or demons that are blowing these trumpets announcing terrible things coming. It is the angels of God: **"The seven angels who had the seven trumpets prepared themselves to sound"** (8:6). These sounds come from heaven. Our Lord, through His angels, will do or allow all these things on earth. That should bring us great comfort. We are not in the hands of hateful terrorists or evil demons. We will continue, even in any tribulation, to be in God's Hands!

4th Angel Sounds:

"And a third of the sun was struck, a third of the moon, and a third of the stars, so that a third of them were darkened: a third of the day did not shine, and likewise the night" (Rev. 8:12). Increasing darkness and less light is a chief characteristic of the worst aspects of the Great Tribulation! "Men loved darkness rather than light because their deeds were evil" (John 3:19). They loved the darkness that hid their sin; now, instead of 12 hours of darkness and 12 of light, there will be 16 hours of darkness and only 8 hours of light. Imagine the sun rising at 6 AM and setting at 2 PM! God will have everybody's attention.

You watch, though! I predict unbelievers will have some excuse, other than the Hand of God, for a lot of this. Trees and grass burning: *"It's the global warming we have warned you about."* A Meteor hitting earth: *"It's just a chance encounter from outer space that scientists have been predicting."* Poisoned waters: *"We warned you about ruining the natural environment."* Long, dark days? *"It's the ozone layer finally wreaking havoc on us!"* They may be able to convince some the remarkable events happening are not God's Hand but wait until a very special angel gives his announcement concerning the last three angels sounding!

The "Woes" Begin

"Woe, woe, woe to the inhabitants of the earth, because of the remaining blasts of the trumpet of the three angels who are about to sound" (8:13). Instead of three "woes," the BBE says, "Trouble, trouble, trouble." The GNT says, "O horror! Horror! How horrible it will be." 8:13 is the verse that helps us understand Chapter Nine.

The trumpet judgments of Chapter Eight were bad enough, but what is next to come is woeful indeed. Here's my prediction…Horrible things begin happening on earth. If the church has not been raptured yet, earthly events will cause great fear to many millions. That fear causes them to turn to the church for answers. And they are turning to a church filled with power and the fire of God, with great faith that God answers prayer!

The greatest revival in history begins or, if already ongoing, will significantly speed up!

Chapter 9

5th and 6th Angels

5th Angel Sounds:

"And he opened the bottomless pit...out of the smoke locusts came upon the earth...they were not given authority to kill them, but to torment them for five months. And their torment was like the torment of a scorpion when it strikes a man" (2-5). At first, it would seem these were actual locusts with stinging power. The closest way to describe the pain is probably like an insect bite. I have been stung by ants and bees and by a wasp (stinging the top of my head!). Stings really hurt! Whatever the actual pain may be, it won't be any fun at all!

When John goes on to describe these beings (8:7-10) we understand these "locusts" are surely symbolic of something else. The description includes… **"like horses,"**… **"tails like scorpions,"**… **"faces of men,"**…**"hair like women's hair."**

Hal Lindsay, in his book "The Late Great Planet Earth," suggested these were possibly symbolic of helicopters. Well, when China invents a helicopter with **"hair like women's hair,"** I'll accept his theory. Otherwise, John just seems to be describing something out of a horror movie which could be symbolic of many things, things which we don't understand clearly yet!

Remember another law of hermeneutics: *"Translate the Bible literally unless it is obviously symbolic."* These weird beings certainly seem symbolic to me, as much of Revelation is! Note, however, that this "woe" will only last five months (a little good news in all of this!).

Then 9:11 tells us these beings are led by a king **"Whose name in Hebrew is Abaddon** (means Destruction) **but in the Greek he has the name Apollyon** (means Destroyer). It is not known for sure who this king of the bottomless pit is, but the fact that it is "an angel" gives some evidence these beings are fallen angels or demons led by an angel.

Throughout history, biblical scholars have tried to interpret the book of Revelation as it might relate to current events (Don't we still do this today?). Some thought Apollyon was referring to the French General Napoleon (From the similarity of their names), wreaking havoc across Europe and Russia. And some thought Hitler was the Antichrist! So, knowing the church's history, we must be humble regarding any claimed present "truths" about the book of Revelation.

9:6 brings out an interesting point about this time: **"In those days men will seek death and will not find it; they will desire to die, and death will flee from them."** Suicide is now viewed by many Americans as an honorable way of escape, even used by teenagers to escape from things like bullying or shaming. This first woe will be so terrible, and so many will want to commit suicide to escape it the Lord is going to have to intervene and stop all these suicides.

It doesn't say how, but I could envision guns misfiring, the body suddenly being able to tolerate 100 Tylenol tablets, or nooses easily breaking! (Angels will be busy bees in that hour! God carefully controls this Tribulation period from heaven!)

The saying *"God is in Control"* has been used to comfort the church through the ages. However, God was not always in control of this out-of-control fallen world. Sometimes evil men were! Yet, it is undoubtedly true that during the fulfillment of the Book of

Revelation, God, with the assistance of His angels, will make sure every line of prophecy is faithfully fulfilled and under His total control! The end times are here?

GOD IS IN CONTROL!

6th Angel Sounds:

"I heard...a voice...saying to the sixth angel... 'Release...the four angels, who had been prepared...to kill a third of mankind.'" (9:15). Four angels are released when the 6th angel sounds. Note for what purpose: "to kill a third of mankind." 9:17, 18 adds: "out of their mouths came" 1. fire...2.smoke... 3. brimstone."

These three things could be literal, of course. But what is scary is the fact these are quite accurate descriptions of the devastation of nuclear weapons! And since one-third of the earth's population would be killed (v. 18), it isn't hard for 21st-century inhabitants to accept this could be a nuclear war! God forbid!

"The rest of mankind, who were not killed by these plagues, did not repent" (9:20). If taken literally, "the rest of mankind" would seem to indicate that the church has already been raptured. Consider a partial list of sins last day earthlings will not repent of...

> 1. "worship (of) demons." Satanism and idolatry are present now but imagine how unbelievers will look to the nether spiritual realm for help during these Tribulation times!

> 2. "Murders." Murdering people for food or just for hatred will be widespread (We are seeing news reports regularly of people killing others for no excusable reason!).

> 3. "Sorceries." According to Vine's Expository Dictionary, this word in Greek is "pharmakia," which primarily signified

the use of drugs, spells, or sorcery. Millions are taking drugs even today to numb the physical or emotional pain of life. So, we certainly could see drug addiction as pandemic! And the rising interest in witchcraft, psychics, hypnotism, palm-reading, fortune-telling, etc., will increase as never before!

4. "Their immorality." Extramarital sex, homosexual marriage, transsexualism, and pornography are already universally deeply rooted. To that we must add prostitution, as women will surely be offering their bodies on street corners for food to feed their children (San Francisco already determined they would not arrest women for soliciting prostitution!).

5. "Their thefts." I predict roving gangs of people robbing and stealing because of food shortages and lost jobs from a devastated world economy! Already, we hear reports of mass, organized store emptying.

The world is indeed facing woes, woes of the nth degree! Yet, I want to encourage you that, referring to the "locusts" unleashed from hell, they will not touch some: **"They were commanded not to harm…but only those men who do not have the seal of God on their foreheads"** (9:4).

This verse could be referring to the 144,000 who were "sealed by God" in 7:7. If it is referring to that group and that group only, this would bring to mind four propositions:

1. The church has already been raptured

2. There are only 144,000 true Christians still left on the earth

3. Only the 144,000 Jews are protected

Or, and the one I prefer…

4. 144,000 is one of God's perfect numbers and does not mean exactly this amount will be marked, but any and all who qualify will be! And this could include many millions! If so, I pray to be among them! Verse four seems to be a reference to the 144,000 of 7:7. But, "rightly dividing the word of truth," consider a few other biblical references…

"The Blood shall be a SIGN for you on the houses where you are, And when I see the blood I will pass over you; and the plague shall not be on you to destroy you when I strike the land of Egypt" (Exodus 12:23). Couldn't this foreshadow the terrible judgments of the tribulation with those covered in the Blood being, in essence, sealed in their foreheads and thus supernaturally protected?

God had seen enough of Israel's abominations, and so He instructed the prophet to tell those who had charge over the city to (Ezekiel 8:4-6): "**Go through the midst of the city…and put a mark on the foreheads of the men who sigh and cry over all the abominations that are done within it** ("Sighing and crying"—aren't Christians doing that? If not, surely, if Great Tribulation developments appear, they will!). **Go…through the city and kill…utterly slay old and young men, maidens and little children and women; but… DO NOT COME NEAR ANYONE ON WHOM IS THE MARK!**"

There are only two marks on the foreheads of end times men and women—the mark of the beast and the mark of God!

Which mark will you bear?

Chapter 10

The Mystery Revealed

"In the days of the sounding of the 7th angel...the mystery of God would be finished" (Rev. 10:7). We don't know if people on the earth will hear these trumpets blown by angels or if the sounds are only signals to those in heaven preparing to control earthly events. But, oh, what terrible things will be happening when the first six angels sound their trumpets! Yet, following them comes an announcement as the...

7th Angel sounds:

"The angel... lifted up his right hand to heaven and swore... that there should be delay no longer" (10:5, 6). Something that had been long delayed was about to happen. This calls to mind Matt. 24:48, where a wicked servant says, "My Lord delays His coming."

Then the angel explains what had been delayed in 10:7: "**The mystery of God would be finished, as He declared to His servants the prophets.**" And what mystery is the angel talking about? Rightly dividing the Word of truth, we go to 1 Cor. 15:51, 52: "Behold, I tell you a mystery: We shall not all sleep, but we shall all be changed— in a moment, in the twinkling of an eye, at the last trumpet. For the trumpet will sound, and the dead will be raised incorruptible, and we shall be changed." There is little question these verses speak of the coming of the Lord and our rapture to heaven. Rev. 10:14 and 1 Cor. 15:51 both speak of the same "mystery" because Revelation chapter 8-10 show seven Trumpets sounded (trumpeted) by seven angels. The sounding of the 7th angel is the last time the book of Revelation speaks of an angel using a trumpet. 1 Cor. 15:51 says the Lord will come "at the last trumpet."

Thus, the seventh angel's sounding is surely the same announcement (made by a trumpet) as that sounded at Christ's return! And since the Lord doesn't come until the sounding of the Seventh Trumpet, this is scriptural evidence the church will still be upon the earth during the first six trumpets.

If these were the only verses we had, this would, in my view, be irrefutable proof Christians will be in at least part of the Great Tribulation. Also, in case you didn't take note when we were in Revelation Chapter 6, it would be hard to debate that 6:12-17 is not talking about the second coming of Christ. Again, this was revealed BEFORE the sounding of the seven angels in chapters 8-10. I repeat, Revelation is not written sequentially! It is written discursively! My brother and sister, prepare your heart and life to possibly *BE HERE for some of the terrible events coming upon the earth!*

Yet, hallelujah, we still have our great hope that the Lord will, by the Seventh Trumpet, without any further delay (Though now over 2000 years!), wrap up the "mystery" of the ages by taking us to heaven and then back to Earth again for His eternal kingdom reign (and ours with Him!).

Seven Thunders

"Now when the seven thunders uttered their voices, I was about to write; but I heard a voice from heaven saying to me, "Seal up the things which the seven thunders utter, and do not write them.'" (10:4). This is reminiscent of Paul's reprt in 2 Cor. 12:2-4 when he "was caught up to the third heaven... and heard inexpressible words, which it is not lawful for a man to utter." Both John and Paul show us there are things yet to be revealed that could not even be included in the scriptures! What they are and why they couldn't be shown to the church we can only speculate. But God gave us a good clue...

"That in the ages to come he might show the exceeding riches of his grace in his kindness toward us through Christ Jesus" (Eph. 2:7). What a future is in store: "exceeding riches"..."grace"..."kindness"... (and I especially like this part) "TOWARD US." There are so many glorious things awaiting us in eternity that we should not be worried about relatively brief tribulation hardships, which will but serve to remind us of the very soon coming of our Lord!

Honey

A book was put in the hands of John. The angel told him, "Take and eat it; and it will make your stomach bitter, but it will be as sweet as honey in your mouth...You must prophesy again about many peoples, nations, tongues, and kings" (10:9-11).

The same thing happened to another prophet in Ezekiel chapter three. Many prophetic words God gives can have a very bitter result. We see in John's prophecy some things that are very hard to digest and could make one full of fear and dread. At first, the thought of being here during part of the Great Tribulation was depressing. But, as I have subsequently studied, read about, and heard of the wonderful revival ahead of us and the reports from many who have died and visited heaven and come back to describe how wonderful it is, I have discovered an encouraging "sweetness" amongst the bitter.

John's "bitter" prophecies had a "sweet taste" to his mouth—

sweet as honey! Compare with Psalm 119:103: "How sweet are Your words to my taste, *Sweeter* than honey to my mouth!" We need to be so in love with the Lord and to have so learned to live with an ongoing awareness of His love towards us that even the worst prophetic "words" from God, though bitter to the flesh, can nevertheless be "sweeter than honey" to our mouths. "Taste and see that the Lord is good" (Ps. 34:8). The Lord never changes. He will always be good! He won't suddenly become a cruel ogre for seven years at the end of the age! He will always be good to us and His Word to us will always be sweet!

A time of bitterness and a time of sweetness may soon be upon us. How will you handle it? It is truly the half-empty, half-full principle. What do we do any of these trumpet judgments are happening around us? Jesus told us EXACTLY what to do in Luke 21:26-28: "**Men's heart (will be) failing them from fear and expectation of those things which are coming on the earth, for the powers of the heavens will be shaken. Then they will see the Son of Man coming...Now when these things BEGIN** (Notice we may see at least the beginning of the Great Tribulation!) **to come to pass, Look up and lift up <u>YOUR</u>** (Remember, Jesus was saying this to His followers) **heads, because your redemption draws near.**"

We may see the rise of the Antichrist, but we aren't looking for that and bowing our heads in fear. Instead, we are looking for the Lord to break through the clouds of glory! Thus, regardless of events on earth, we are lifting our heads in joyous praise because we know we'll soon begin our eternal journey with Him!

Temporary bitterness leads to eternal honey!

Chapter 11

Finish Your Testimony

"Now when they finish their testimony" (Rev. 11:7). Revelation 11 describes the ministry of the "two witnesses," which requires 14 verses of the chapter, so we know this is a VERY important event! Who are these two witnesses? They are prophets, and 11:4 tells us they are the prophetic fulfillment of Zech. 4:11-14: "**These are the two olive trees and the two lampstands standing before the God of the whole earth.**"

We don't know for sure who they are, but many believe they are Enoch and Elijah (who never died and were translated into heaven, so now they come back to earth once more to minister until they die a martyr's death). Their ministry lasts three-and-a-half years (10:2), and their work seems to run concurrently with the Antichrist's control of the Temple, which is also three and a half years. The Temple "**court has been given to the Gentiles. And they will tread the holy city underfoot for 42 months**" (10:3). This is undoubtedly in fulfillment of Daniel's prophecy in 8:9-11 describing the Antichrist invasion of Israel!

The witnesses' ministry is centered in Jerusalem, perhaps to help hold at bay the Antichrist's success. They bring global catastrophes

(11:6) as they are given extraordinary powers, including stopping the rain from falling, turning water to blood, causing plagues, and even tormenting the people on earth (11:10). Could these witnesses, through their God-given power, simply be fulfilling the trumpet announcements of the six angels?

To protect themselves, the two witnesses are given an extraordinary power—fire comes out of their mouths to destroy their enemies (11:5). Despite their fiery defense, the forces of the Antichrist will finally succeed in killing them. While their bodies lie in the street, people worldwide will celebrate their death (By seeing it on TV and on their cell phones?).

But the Lord will resurrect them after three and a half days. (Do you think three and a half is an important number in the last days? It must be!). Simultaneously, there will be a great earthquake, destroying one-tenth of Jerusalem, causing 7,000 deaths (1/10th, 7,000...literal or symbolic?). The witnesses' resurrection viewed and replayed again and again, and the devastation of the earthquake brings a strong reaction from the world: "**the rest were afraid**" (11:13).

Then, the world does something surprising. They "**gave glory to the God of heaven**" (11:13). **This doesn't mean they lifted their hands and praised the Lord. It simply means they stood in awe of God's hand and realized only He should be given credit for these fantastic events: a resurrection and an earthquake (two events that also happened in Jerusalem when Christ rose from the grave!).**

These three and a half years of an Antichrist reign (who will surely be continually wreaking havoc) and the calamities caused by the two witnesses are likely included in "the second woe" in 10:14. The events of the "second woe" are in 9:13-11:13. After "**The second woe is past. Behold, the third woe is coming quickly**" (11:14). The third woe is not defined, but since the next chapter focuses on Satan's fall from heaven and his world-wide rampage against God's people, that is, by any definition, certainly a woe!

Also in the context of the third woe is the mention of the coming of Christ, which is a repetition of the event announced by the trumpeting of the seventh angel in 10:7. (Again, do not read all Revelation sequentially!). "And the seventh angel sounded. And there were loud voices in heaven, saying, 'The kingdoms of this world have become the kingdoms of His Christ, and He shall reign forever and ever.'"

My favorite verse in chapter 11 is: "Now when they finish their testimony" (v.10:7). The two witnesses will supernaturally be kept alive until they have finished their work on earth, which is an exact number of days, 1260! This brings to mind Deut. 30:20 (KJV): "Love the Lord thy God, that thou mayest obey his voice, and that thou mayest cleave unto him: for he is thy life and the length of thy days." If you obey His voice and are "cleaving" to Him, no matter how difficult these last days ahead are, the Lord intends to help you finish the work you are called to do in the length of days (just the right amount for you personally) He has planned for you!

Jesus only lived 33 years on earth, yet He could say, "I have finished the work which You gave me to do" (Jn. 17:4). Jesus finished his testimony! Paul wrote concerning John the Baptist: "as John was finishing his course." John finished his testimony! Paul "finished (his) course" (2 Tim. 4:7). Paul finished his testimony. Our Hebrews 11 cloud of witnesses is our example. And then... *The two witnesses finished their testimony!*

Oh, I want to finish my testimony, too, don't you? I am willing to stay longer on this earth, in spite of the calamities and persecution going on around me, if I can testify, pray, and preach the gospel until I finish the work God has called me to do!

"You are immortal until you fulfill your destiny."

No antichrist forces, no mark of the beast, no famine, plague, or calamity can keep you from God's purpose for putting you on this earth "for such a time as this."

Let the above witnesses be a great inspiration to you today! You can do this! They finished their testimony. You can yours also!

Believe it! Confess it!

I will finish my testimony!

Chapter 12

Hell Breaks Loose!

> "The devil has come down to you, having great wrath because he knows that he has a short time" (Rev. 12:12).

Revelation 12 is a very interesting chapter. It gives us a panoramic view of the work of Satan from the beginning of creation through the very last days.

In 12:1-5, we see a metaphor for Israel, the birth of Christ, Satan trying to kill Jesus at his birth, and Jesus' ascension to heaven.

"His (the dragon, Satan) tail drew a third of the stars of heaven and threw them to the earth" (12:4). This is how we know one-third of the angels fell with Satan.

The Bible doesn't tell us specifically when Satan "threw" his (stars) angels to earth. It happened before Christ's birth, for Jesus said in Luke 10:18: **"I saw Satan fall like lightning from heaven."** It could have happened right after the creation of the earth, after man's creation, or maybe after man's fall. The earth then became the principal abode of the devil. Paul called the devil **"the god of this** world" (2 Cor. 4:4) and "the prince of the power of the air" (Eph. 2:2). And Jesus called him "**The prince of this world**" (John 12:31).

Even though Satan "fell from heaven," he still was allowed some access to heaven, as we see in Job chapters 1 and 2. Rev. 12:7 tells us about a war in heaven between the devil and his angels and God's holy angels. Satan loses, and he and his angels are "**cast to earth**" and "**cast down.**" You might be thinking, *"Well, I thought earth was already primarily Satan's abode."* It was, but after this war, Satan will no longer be allowed to enter heaven or before God's throne and will have to stay on this planet.

It is such a blessing that of all the things the Word could have said about Satan's evil work, it mentions he "**accused them before God day and night**" (12:10). Foundational to power in the Christian life is the understanding of our complete forgiveness of sin, of our righteous standing before a holy God, of our right to enter His presence boldly in prayer, and to lift holy hands toward heaven in praise without wrath or doubting! "**There is therefore now no condemnation to those who are in Christ**" (Rom. 8:1).

Satan has learned after millennia of experience that condemnation, guilt, shame, and a sense of unworthiness are his most potent weapons to keep God's people from witnessing with boldness, from praying with power, and from serving with joy as a "king and priest" of God! Thus, this "anti-ministry" of the devil virtually ends in one fell swoop in Rev. 12! I personally believe this "cast down" to earth means Satan and his fallen angels will basically be bound to the planet by gravity, just like we are. This is when Satan enters the Antichrist (like he entered Judas) and begins his earthly reign (Not as a red-horned beast depicted in drawings and movies) but hidden in the human body of the Antichrist, who is eventually worshiped by the earth.

In 10:13-16, we see after Satan is "**cast to the earth,**" he will try to destroy the Israelites. God will supernaturally protect His people from a Satanic flood "**spewed out of his mouth**" (Symbolic? Likely). When Satan is unsuccessful in destroying Israel as a nation of people, He then goes "**to make war with the rest of her offspring** (note that word!), **who keep the commandment of God and have the testimony of Jesus Christ**" (10:17).

This verse may seem to speak of the Jewish converts still on the earth after the church is raptured. But remember what Paul taught: "**If you are Christ's, then you are Abraham's seed, and heirs according to the promise**" (Galatians 3:29). "Seed" means "offspring," so this could suggest a war against not just Israel but also the church.

Regardless, in 12:11, we are given a glorious promise that both the church today, the church tomorrow, and any converted last-day Jews can claim when it comes to any war against the devil: "**They overcame him by the blood of the Lamb and by the word of their testimony, and they did not love their lives (even) to the death.**" Let me rephrase that verse in a way that should uplift you: *"Because they understood the power of the blood of Christ, and stood fast to their confession of faith, and because they were willing to boldly hold on to that faith, even when it could cost them their life..."THEY OVERCOME HIM!"*

For a season, the earth will experience the wrath of Satan. That is certainly not a pleasant thought. Nevertheless, if you are troubled about tribulations you may be going through today or the Great Tribulation, you may have to endure tomorrow, meditate on this truth:

You will overcome him!

Chapter 13

42 Difficult Months

"He was given authority to continue for forty-two months (13:5).

Chapter 13 fulfills what Paul prophesied in 2 Thess. 2:3, 4, the time when the Antichrist (also known as "the beast") rises to power: "The man of sin is revealed, the son of perdition, who opposes and exalts himself above all that is called God or that is worshiped, so that he sits as God in the temple of God, showing himself that he is God."

Of the Antichrist, 13:1, 2 says: "The dragon (Satan) gave him his power, his throne, and his great authority." When Jesus walked the earth, Satan offered Him the same power and authority. Still, Jesus refused: "The devil…showed Him all the kingdoms of the world…and said to Him, "All this authority I will give You, and their glory; for this has been delivered to me, and I give it to whomever I wish. Therefore, if You will worship before me, all will be Yours" (Luke 4:6, 7).

Aren't you glad Jesus responded to this temptation with, "Get behind me, Satan." (We must say the same thing if we are ever commanded to worship the beast)

A remarkable Satan-chosen man, the Antichrist (called "**a son of perdition,**" the same name Jesus gave Judas in John 17:12), will one day gladly accept Satan's offer to rule all the kingdoms of the world! Apparently, somebody will try to assassinate the Antichrist (13:3) but will be unsuccessful (Be on the lookout for a highly visible leader being shot or stabbed in the head and yet survive!).

Then, we're told a chilling thing: "All the world marveled and followed the beast" (13:3). "**They worshipped the dragon who gave authority to the beast**" (13:4). When people worship idols they are actually worshipping the demons behind that idol: "**The things which the Gentiles sacrifice, they sacrifice to devils (demons), and not to God: and I would not that ye should have fellowship with devils**" (1 Cor. 10:20 KJV).

So, Satan would not have to actually manifest himself to be worshipped. However, Satanism may be the most widespread religion in the world at this time, and Satan will get credit finally as "the god of this world" without actually showing up on the scene.

Because of the "strong delusion" of the last days (2 Tim. 2:10-12), a man, the beast, is worshiped as the world boasts, "**Who is like the beast?**" (13:4). God is arranging things to be temporary: "**He was given authority to continue for forty-two months (3½ years!).**"

Are you convinced the Great Tribulation is an actual seven-year period with a great dividing point halfway through it? There is debate about what happens in the first three-and-a-half and the second three-and-a-half. Many believe the rapture takes place in the middle. If you are a "pre-wrath" believer, maybe the second three-and-a-half period begins when Satan is cast to earth and the "woe" of his "wrath" begins. Then, at some point, the Lord rescues His church before God's wrath is poured out on everyone else.

Next might be my least favorite verse in the Bible: "**It was granted to him** (the Antichrist) **to make war with the saints and to overcome them**" (13:7). This could be short-lived, but an all-out attack on Christians, Jews, or anybody without his mark before the rapture.

When it says Satan will "overcome them," this is not a contradiction of the promise that we will "overcome" the devil (12:12). Rather, it probably means the church will be under such great persecution and political attacks that it will almost be shut down physically. (Perhaps super churches emptied, Christian TV programming gone, Bible Colleges nearly shuttered, secret meetings in homes the "norm" for the church?)

Christianity is now the most persecuted group in the world! We see Satan is already trying to shut down the church in communist and Muslim countries. Thus, it shouldn't be hard at all to envision a day soon when the devil will bring severe persecution to every country of the world, including America! Yet, we are promised we can overcome Satan's every temptation and will "**overcome the world**" (1 John 5:4). Even though Satan may put some of us in jail or even to death, we still overcome him (Just like Jesus overcame death and the devil when He rose from the grave!).

One day, our nation's global influence will finally end: "**the whole world** (That includes America, doesn't it?) **followed the beast**" (10:4). America's media seems to be leading the way. Several years back, you surely noticed that the liberal TIME MAGAZINE chose Greta Thunberg, an angry, uneducated, but eloquent teenager, as their "Person of the Year." The far left considers her an instrument to push the Green Agenda. The prophet Isaiah warned us about people like Greta in Isa. 3:12 (KJV), "**As for my people, children are their oppressors, and women rule over them. O my people, they which lead thee cause thee to err, and destroy the ways of thy paths.**"

A child/woman has become a chief spokesman for fanatical

environmentalism! Her doctrine is being fed to her by others! Remember, she was A HIGH SCHOOL TEENAGER who dropped out of school to fulfill her mission! If the "Green New Deal" were made the law of the land, this would indeed "cause us to err" by depleting our economic health and **"destroy the way of thy paths"** by indebting our children and grandchildren with an insurmountable debt that could destroy the prosperous American "way" of life forever!

The Antichrist is only allowed to reign for 42 months. Could this refer to the first half of the Great Tribulation as a time of gaining power and amassing the nations to do his bidding? Then comes the rapture. In the second 42 months, while we are in heaven, the wrath of God will be poured out on the Antichrist Kingdom, which can do nothing against the plagues in chapter 16. Then God allows one more satanic conspiracy as the Antichrist somehow deceives many and gathers an international army for the battle of Armageddon, which we will study in chapter 19.

The work of the Antichrist will not be overnight, as though He quickly flies into Jerusalem and immediately sends out 10 million workers door to door to put every Christian to death. It took Hitler months and even years to take control of surrounding nations, to mark the Jews, and send them to labor camps until he eventually put them to death.

So, it is my hope that we who are not deceived by the rise of the Antichrist may still have months, if not years, to evangelize. I believe God revealed to me that I would! On a positive note... Only 42 months. Think about it. That is a relatively short time compared to our coming 1000-year reign with Christ (12,000 months!). You probably lasted more than 42 months in high school. You may have lasted 48 months or more at a difficult college. Many of you lasted hundreds of months on your difficult job. What, then, are just 42 months of difficulty under the Antichrist? Paul put it in a way we can joyfully confess: "I consider that the sufferings of this present time are not worthy to be compared with the glory which shall be revealed in us" (Romans 8:18).

The Mark

"And he (the Antichrist) causes all, both small and great, rich and poor, free and slave, to receive a mark on their right hand or on their foreheads" (Revelation 13:16). What is the mark? The mark of the beast will one day clearly and forever seal the fate of every person left on earth. It has been argued through the ages what this mark will be. Whatever it is, God's faithful people will indeed not be deceived!

The computer chips now being implanted under the skin of animals and even humans could be a sign of the modus operandi of the mark. 13:18 even tells us that "wisdom" can help us to understand who the beast is and what that mark is: "**Here is wisdom. Let him who has understanding calculate the number of the beast, for it is the number of a man. His number is 666.**" I don't believe it has to be a literal 666. That could be symbolic. But "here is wisdom" must mean some wise man out there has or will soon figure it all out.

God will prepare leaders to let us all know ahead of time how to be prepared. (Maybe through a bestselling book, TBN, CBN, or a quick post on Facebook spread throughout the earth before it is shut down once and for all?). I have often thought about what I would do if they knocked on my door and confronted me with the decision of whether or not to take the mark. If that day comes, I trust the Lord to give me strength to say a resounding "NO!" Many will be deceived or will, like Adam, partake of the fruit knowingly because they don't want to be unable to buy food for their family, or they aren't willing to go to prison or die for their faith! We are shown the greatest decision any generation has ever had to make: "**All who dwell on the earth will** worship him (the beast), whose names have not been written in the Book of Life" (13:8).

To this evangelist, it looks like evangelism will be all but shut down and the saints and the aints will have been "written" up once and for all—their eternal choices having been made.

Rev. 13:11-16 describes the rise of the man, another "beast," who is referred to in 20:10 as **"the false prophet."** He will have people build an image (a statue or idol) to the beast and he will make the image "breathe" and "speak." This image could be stone turned into a living being, like something we've seen in a horror movie. Or it could simply be the most advanced robot ever invented with the most advanced computer brain. The image would be horrifying (but I must admit, interesting) to see.

The false prophet then makes everyone either worship the image, or they will be killed (Reminiscent of the king of Babylon in Daniel 3 demanding that everyone worship his image or be killed). This process could take years. And you may be raptured before they get a chance to knock on your door. Yet, be encouraged; the three Hebrew Children were supernaturally protected despite the fire. Many of us will be supernaturally protected if still here during the Great Tribulation.

With modern technology, it would be impossible for any of us to escape eventual detection by Antichrist police. But, just as it is impossible for a human being to live through a fiery furnace, or for Jesus to escape through a big crowd of people trying to throw him off a cliff, or for an angel to open a locked prison door for Peter to escape, the Lord will easily fulfill the truth of Psalm 18:26: **"To the devious, you will show yourself shrewd."**

God gave Paul many escapes from death until the Lord finally allowed him to become a martyr! Can we believe for the same?

"He who leads into captivity shall go into captivity; he who kills with the sword must be killed with the sword. Here is the

patience and the faith of the saints" (Rev. 13:10). Jeremiah said a very similar thing: **"When he (king of Babylon) comes, he shall strike the land of Egypt and deliver to death those appointed for death, and to captivity those appointed for captivity, and to the sword those appointed for the sword"** (Jer. 43:11). Most translations use the word "destined" instead of "appointed" when describing this time of persecution. I am of the opinion that (rightly dividing the Word), this verse is NOT saying: *"God already predetermined who among us would be imprisoned or become martyrs."* The Antichrist is the one determining this, just as the king of Babylon chose to kill many with sword and to spare others and bring them back to Babylon into "captivity." Many Christians could be imprisoned, and many even killed. The Antichrist will determine that by his own evil intentions. But ultimately God will decide who is hidden, who is imprisoned, and who becomes a martyr. God knows the future, and He will sovereignly decide what happens to each of His children. We could argue this is our destiny.

Yet, I do not believe this scripture is suggesting you and I should just sit around thinking: *"Well, whether or not I become a martyr is up to Him. I'll just sit here and see what happens."* No! Not any more than if you had a heart attack, you would just cavalierly say: *"Well, it's up to God what happens; I am not calling for an ambulance. I am just going to sit around and see if God heals me or not."*

Paul eventually became a martyr for Christ, but that didn't stop him from getting in a basket and lowering himself out of a window to escape persecution! Let's do all we can to survive as long as we can—it isn't rocket science! The reign of the Antichrist, with all the technology (Satellites, drones, cell phone towers, giant internet-controlling companies, and video cameras everywhere), could bring such rapid death that God would have to get involved in the final details of His chosen children's lives.

Think about this: *The average American is photographed (or videotaped) over 70 times a day!* There will NOT be any natural hiding place down here in the final days! Yet, all Christians should find great comfort in knowing our ultimate destiny is not in the hands of the Antichrist, the false prophet, or the devil. No! **"…to GOD, the Lord, belong escapes from death"** (Ps. 68:20 NRSV).

So, because of this **"great tribulation, such as has not been since the beginning of the world"** (Matt. 24:21), we are given an important warning: **"Here is the patience and the faith of the saints"** (13:10). The NRSV puts it: **"Here is a call for the endurance and faith of the saints."**

This should remind us of Jesus' end time warning: **"He who endures to the end shall be saved"** (Matt. 24:13). Considering all these events in chapter 13, it is no wonder there will be a **"great falling away"** during the rise of the Antichrist (2 Thess. 2:3).

Endure temptations, tribulations, and persecutions now. Keep your faith and trust in the Lord now. Then you will be secured by His power and love in that final hour: **"And through your faith, God is protecting you by his power until you receive this salvation, which is ready to be revealed on the last day for all to see"** (1 Peter 1:5 NLT).

Here is another wonderful promise: **"Because you have obeyed my command to endure, I will keep you SAFE during the time of testing which is coming to the whole world to test those living on earth"** (Rev. 2:10 GW).

"Safe" can mean safe from starvation, safe from weather catastrophes, safe from prison, or even safe from death. Whatever happens, we are promised in the "game of life" that when we at last reach home base, God, the Umpire of the Universe, will say to us,

"Safe!"

Chapter 14

The 144,000

> "Behold, a Lamb standing on Mt. Zion, and with Him 144,000, having His Father's name written on their foreheads" (14:1).

Rev. 14:1-5 tells us of an elite group of people previously referred to in 7:1-8 where it said that from these 144,000, 12,000 were chosen from each of the 12 tribes of Israel. The fact is that the tribes of the Jewish nation are probably so inbred that, after millennia, it is likely every Jew would now have most of the tribes in his bloodline (and often a few gentiles!), yet the text says, "12,000 from the tribe of Benjamin," etc. Of course, God could take those with 1/1,024 and call them Benjaminites if He wanted to.

Paul wrote that we have been "grafted in" to the vine of Israel (Rom. 11:17), so this could include gentile believers! Other biblical texts justify Christians being brought into a Jewish covenant relationship: "Gentiles used to be outsiders. You were called "uncircumcised heathens" by the Jews, who were proud of their circumcision, even though it affected only their bodies and not their hearts. In those days you were living apart from Christ. You were excluded from citizenship among the people of Israel, and you did not know the covenant promises God had made to them. You lived in this world without God and without hope. But now you have been united with Christ Jesus. Once you were far away from God, but now you have been brought near to him through the blood of Christ...So now you Gentiles are no longer strangers and foreigners. You are citizens along with all of God's holy people. You are members of God's family" (Ephesians 2:11, 12, 13, 19).

"For he is not a Jew who is one outwardly, nor is circumcision that which is outward in the flesh; but he is a Jew who is one inwardly; and circumcision is that of the heart, in the Spirit, not in the letter" (Romans 2:28, 29). "They are not all Israel who are of Israel, nor are they all children because they are the seed of Abraham; but, 'In Isaac your seed shall be called.' That is, those who are the children of the flesh (physical Jews) are not the children of God; but the children of the promise are counted as the seed" (Romans 9:6-8). "Jerusalem which now is, and is in bondage with her children—but the Jerusalem above is free, which is the mother of us all...we brethren, as Isaac was, are children of promise" Gal. 4:25, 26, 28). "(We Believers) are the circumcision, who worship God in the Spirit" (Philippians 3:3). The verses above allow us to say believing gentiles are now "God's chosen people" so to speak.

Most Evangelical Christians believe in both "Spiritual Israel" (the church) and "Physical Israel" (the Jewish nation worldwide). Many promises in the Bible can only be claimed by believers in Christ. However, some promises indicate the Lord still has plans for national Israel, and in the last days, He will do a work of grace among physical Jews. A great proof-text for this is in Romans 11:25, 26: "hardening in part has happened to Israel until the fullness of the Gentiles has come in. And so all Israel will be saved, as it is written: 'The

Deliverer will come out of Zion, and He will turn away ungodliness from Jacob.'"

Yes, God indeed has a last-day plan to revive his people, Israel. Note that v. 25 says this hardening continues **"until the fullness of the Gentiles has come in."** Some argue after all the gentiles that are going to be saved are saved and then raptured, the Lord will start dealing with Israel again and this is what the 144,000 are about. They could be right, but because of the scriptures proving that Christians are also Israelites, I believe it is likely otherwise. Romans 2:29 says **"he is a Jew who is one inwardly."** So, your confession in these end times can be,

"I am a Jew on the inside, so I can claim all the grace, protection, promises, and blessings promised to Israel."

The Warriors

"I looked, and behold, a Lamb standing on Mount Zion, and with Him one hundred and forty-four thousand" (Revelation 14:1). 144,000 could be an actual exact count or symbolic since it is a "perfect" number (12,000 times 12,000). Twelve is one of God's perfect numbers (Consider the 12 patriarchs and the 12 apostles). A thousand is also one of God's perfect numbers (Consider the 1,000-year reign of Christ on earth). Here is what I hope this symbolic number is referring to…

The 144,000 are a special end time army that God calls, seals and mightily uses for a season during the last days.

This is just a theory (We would be wise to consider almost every "interpretation" of the Book of Revelation as a theory!). Even if it is wrong, and the 144,000 are Jewish and do not include any of us, we can still learn something about the character of God and the character of the people He chooses from this elite group.

If I am not one of the 144,000, I want to at least be worthy of God "sealing" me and setting me apart for His end time purposes. So, with that in mind, let's see what kind of person God includes in that special (eight verses in chapter 7 and five verses in chapter 14 are devoted to them) end time army!

The Lamb (Jesus) is seen standing on Mount Zion. Mount Zion could be the heavenly city, or it could just refer to Jerusalem. But further examination of this chapter provides evidence this is a view of the 144,000 after they are translated to heaven. These 144,000 are special because...

> 1. "The Father's name written on their foreheads" (14:1). *These will NOT receive the mark of the beast, and you and I must also not receive that mark if we want to make heaven our home!*

> 2. "They sang…a new song before the throne…and no one could learn that song except the 144,000" (14:3). *These are worshippers who love to sing in God's presence. Do you?*

> 3. "They were redeemed from the earth" (14:3). *They were raptured to heaven.*

> 4. "These are the ones who were not defiled with women" (14:4). The word "defiled" is moluua in the Greek. Moluua means, *"soiled, smeared with mud or filth."* In the Old Testament, priests who had defiled their garments had to clean them before they could do their priestly duties. As **"kings and priests"** (Rev. 1:6), we must keep our garments undefiled, white, and clean. Lust, pornography, fornication, and adultery are sins of our age. "Out of the heart proceed evil thoughts… fornications…These are the things that defile a man" (Matt. 15:19, 20).

Satan is fighting so hard to keep Christians in bondage to impurity. He wants to so defile them that God can't use them! Jesus also said, "**Those things which proceed out of the mouth come from the heart, and they defile a man**" (Matt. 15:18). No wonder movies today are so filled with graphic language. Satan wants to defile our mouths and minds.

5. **"for they are virgins"** (14:4). I do not believe this means they were only single-committed people. Rather, even married people, because of the purity of their relationship with their mate and the purity of their mind, in God's eyes, are considered a "virgin" and can be among the 144,000. Married Christians can be virgins: "**I have espoused you to one husband, that I may present you as a chaste virgin to Christ**" (2 Cor. 11:2 KJV). *Are you a "chaste virgin to Christ?"*

Walk in purity before your Lord in these last days. It will not only mean you help secure your salvation but might even make you a candidate for a last-day 144,000 army of holy men and women warriors!

6. **"These are the ones who follow the Lamb wherever He goes"** (14:4). Following Jesus is the requirement of the 144,000. And OBEDIENCE is the number one requirement for any man or woman God uses! (Thus, Satan, in his wrath, in 12:17, made "**war with (those)…who keep the commandments of God.**"

Paul wrote in Romans 1:5: "**We have received grace…for obedience to the faith.**" Grace without obedience is not the "faith" of the gospel! I fear many teaching or believing an "easy believism," emphasizing God's love and grace without the balance of repentance, overcoming besetting sins, and obeying the gospel are playing into the hand of the devil.

When Paul was preaching to Felix, the governor, he didn't just tell him, *"God loves you, and Jesus wants to come into your heart and save you by faith."* Instead, Paul, **"reasoned about righteousness, self-control, and the judgment to come"** (Acts 24:25). Did Paul's message make Felix feel warm, fuzzy, and loved by God? No! **"Felix was AFRAID and answered, 'Go away for now."** I use fear as one motivator in my altar calls because "The fear of the Lord is the beginning of wisdom" (Prov. 9:10). We obey God because we fear Him, and we fear, like Felix, "the judgment to come."

7. **"These were redeemed from among men"** (14:4). God chooses people from among average joes ("from among men") who make the grade. *Do you make the grade?*

8. **"Being first fruits to God and to the Lamb"** (14:4). The first fruits in the Old Testament were the first harvested vegetables or fruits from the crops. Some believe in two raptures: The "first fruits" (they deserve not to have to go through the tribulation), and the rest of the redeemed are raptured later (they are Purified by the tribulation). This is but another theory.

One thing we know. Whether elite Jews, or symbolic of many sanctified chosen Christians, these 144,000 are surely the crème de la crème of the end times.

9. **"And in their mouth was found no guile (falsehood)"** (14:5). It is amazing how common lying has become. We need to take note of Rev. 21:8: **"All liars shall have their part in the lake which burns with fire."** Christians must always "speak the truth in love" (Eph. 4:15), especially if they want to be a

soldier God chooses for His army. I say, *"Draft me, Lord!"*

10. **"For they are without fault before the throne of God"** (14:5). This is NOT saying they had to perfectly overcome every sin. I don't think any man has ever done that this side of heaven! It means they have learned to appropriate by faith the faultlessness that gives us the privilege to stand before God: **"(He) is able to keep you from falling, and to present you faultless before the presence of his glory with exceeding joy"** (Jude 24).

Here is a glorious promise: **"You who once were alienated and enemies in our mind by wicked works, yet now He has reconciled, in the body of His flesh through death, to present you holy, and blameless (faultless)...in His sight"** (Col. 1:22). However, there is one caveat for this privilege of "being without fault" which Paul makes clear in verse 23: **"If you continue in the faith, grounded and steadfast, and are not moved away from the hope of the gospel."** *You will not be among the redeemed if you join the great falling away.*

In the 144,000, we have seen the Father's heart. He wants to write His name on our foreheads, teach us a new song, not one just anyone can sing, and walk with purity of heart and mouth before Him. And He wants us to obey Him every day!

After reading all the above, don't you want to make your Father happy with your life? If so, get in His presence. Sing new songs before Him. Ask Jesus to give you guidance now and especially in the difficult days to come. The 144,000 show us in 14:4 how:

"follow the Lamb wherever He goes"

Two Angelic Reapings

The Saved

Rev. 14:14 then speaks of a harvest that sure sounds to me like the rapture (and it is smack dab in the middle of the Tribulation!). An angel crying with a loud voice said, "**Thrust in your sickle and reap, for the time has come for You to reap, for the harvest of the earth is ripe**" (14:15). Matt. 13:39 is a companion verse: "**the harvest is the end of the age and the reapers are the angels.**"

The Unsaved

Then there is another kind of harvest, not of believers, but of unbelievers in 14:18, 19: "**Thrust in your sharp sickle and gather the clusters of the vine of the earth…So the angel thrust his sickle into the earth and gathered the vine of the earth, and threw it into the great winepress of the wrath of God.**"

The angels will remove the tares from the wheat as Jesus foretold in Matt. 13:30!

Which reaping will you be in?

Chapter 15

The Victory

"I saw...seven angels having the seven
last plagues, for in them the wrath of
God is complete" (Rev. 15:1).

Revelation 15 is the shortest chapter in the New Testament yet one of the most important. It reveals events in heaven just before God's wrath on a Christ-rejecting world "is complete." 15:2: "And I saw something like a sea of glass mingled with fire, and those who have the victory over the beast, over his image and over his mark and over the number of his name, standing on the sea of glass." This describes a scene in heaven of a certain group of redeemed saints. God gives special honor to martyrs and faithful ones who hold steady to the course for this most difficult time in history.

"I saw them...that had gotten the victory over the beast' (KJV). The NRSV says they "had conquered the beast." This is not speaking about those who were raptured before the beast rose to power! You can't conquer an enemy without fighting him. You can't get "the victory" over an opponent you have never faced! Then it adds they also gained another victory: **"over his image and over his mark."** They got the victory by refusing to take the mark!

"And they sing the song of Moses" (15:3). You can read more about this song in Exodus 15:1-19. Moses could be the most important man in history. That heaven would honor Moses by singing his song instead of David's song or Paul's song, I think, speaks volumes!

"Then one of the four living creatures gave to the seven angels seven golden bowls full of the wrath of God" (15:7). This proves the bowls poured out in chapter 16 contain manifestations of the wrath of God.

"The temple was filled with smoke from the glory of God and from His power, and no one was able to enter the temple till the seven plagues...were completed" (15:8). This is a very mysterious Scripture. Why aren't the redeemed allowed in the Temple during this event? What is going on inside that temple? I suggest it is a secret meeting, like a closed-door cabinet meeting of our President, discussing and preparing for war with his generals and highest aides.

This could be when the Father and the Son commune in an intimate discussion and finalize plans for the earth. These are things only the Son, who paid such a dear price to redeem mankind, is worthy to share with the Father. Also, remember even Jesus didn't know the hour when He would be returning to the earth, but only the Father! **"But of that day and hour no one knows, neither the angels in heaven, nor the Son, but only the Father"** (Mark 13:32). After communing in private with the Father, do you think Jesus then knew the exact hour? It sure makes sense to me! There are a few verses from chapter 15 we need to personally consider...

> 1. **"They had gotten the victory over the beast"** (15:2). Have you gotten the victory over the beast of present sins and demonic strongholds in your life? Now is surely the time to

gain that victory. Because, Jesus warned: "If they do these things in the green wood, what will be done in the dry?" (Luke 23:31). This is a metaphor that basically means: *If you can't rise above your circumstances in relatively "green" (prosperous, peaceful times) times, will you really be able to "get the victory" if the "dry" (famine, scarcity, or even tribulation) comes to your life?*

If you can do it now, you can be confident you'll also be able to do it (if you happen to still be around) at the time of the beast. Get any needed victory in the present tense so, if required, it may one day be said of you in the past perfect tense: **"They had gotten the victory."**

2. **"They sing"** (15:3). Do you sing to the Lord often? Do you sing in your devotionals? Do you live joyfully daily with a song in your heart? If you don't, you haven't yet learned one of the most important keys to victory in a time when the entire world will have lost its song forever!

So, start now with a renewed commitment to overcome any "beast" (sin or demonic stronghold) in your life. My fellow victorious one,

"Sing!"

Chapter 16

A Done Deal

> "I heard a loud voice from the temple saying to the 7 angels, 'Go and pour out the bowls of the wrath of God on the earth'" (16:1).

Chapter 16 is full of terrible events, described as "bowls" poured out from seven angels. They are called, **"the bowls of the wrath of God."** That is a scary thought, but I believe we will be safe in heaven before all these events occur. Again, Paul promised us: **"God has not appointed us to wrath"** (1 Thess. 5:9). Even if we were still here on earth, the "bowls of wrath" are not "appointed" for us! Hallelujah! When each of the seven angels pours out his bowl, there are spectacularly uncommon results…

> 1st Bowl: **"a foul and loathsome sore came upon the men who had the mark of the beast and those who worshipped his image"** (16:2).

> 2nd Bowl: **"the sea…became blood as of a dead man; and every living creature in the sea died"** (16:3).

3rd Bowl: "the rivers, springs of water...became like blood" (16:4).

4th Bowl: "men were scorched with great heat" (16:9).

5th Bowl: "the throne of the beast, and his kingdom became full of darkness; and they gnawed their tongues because of the pain" (16:10).

6th Bowl: "I saw three unclean spirits like frogs coming out of the mouth of the dragon, out of the mouth of the beast, and...the false prophet. For they are spirits of demons, performing signs, which go out to the kings of the earth and of the whole world, to gather them to the battle of that great day of God Almighty...And they gathered them together to the place called in Hebrew, Armageddon" (16:12-14, 16).

At the end of the Great Tribulation, the Antichrist, with the help of demons, gathers "the whole world" together for the battle of Armageddon (This happens in chapter 19). Then, evidence that Revelation is NOT written sequentially is shown by what happens at the...

7th Bowl: "And every island disappeared, and all the mountains were leveled" (16:20 NLT). The fall of Babylon, described in chapter 18, happens in 16:19. And yet what happens in 16:20 could surely speak of nothing but the end of the world!

These judgments will parallel the ten plagues that came on the ancient Egyptians before the Israelites were delivered and taken to the Promised Land. View the following comparison between the seven angels' bowls and the Egyptian plagues ...

1. "a foul and loathsome sore came upon the men" (16:2). In Egypt it was boils that came upon them (Ex 9:8, 9).

2. "the sea...became blood...the rivers and springs of... became blood" (16:3). In Egypt, the water was turned to blood (Ex. 7:19).

3. (The beast's) "**kingdom became full of darkness**" (16:10). In Egypt, darkness covered the land—a darkness "you could feel" (Ex. 10:21).

4. "**great hail from heaven fell upon men**" (16:21). In Egypt a very heavy hail fell from heaven (Ex. 19:18).

Starting with the fourth plague (flies), the Lord gave a wonderful promise in Exodus 8:22, 23: "**I will set apart the land of Goshen, in which My people dwell, that no swarms of flies shall be there, in order that you may know that I am the Lord in the midst of the land. I will make a difference between My people and your people.**"

God also protected the livestock of Israel from the animal disease plague: "**The Lord will make a difference between the livestock of Israel and livestock of Egypt. So, nothing shall die of all that belongs to the children of Israel**" (Ex. 9:4).

When the plague of hail fell upon Egypt: "**In the land of Goshen, where the children of Israel were, there was no hail**" (Ex. 9:26).

A "**thick darkness**" fell on Egypt (Ex. 10:23) "**but all the children of Israel had light in their dwellings.**"

Is the historical fact that Israel, along with the Egyptians, experienced some of the first plagues a sign we believers will also experience some of the first plagues? We must at least consider that possibility. There are some who are convinced Christians will still be here on earth during a season when the wrath of God is poured out. But, even if we are actually in heaven, the Lord still wanted us to know about these things coming on earth. (If not to be prepared personally, to understand God will not forsake His Children and does not lumpsum their welfare with the world's. "Against none of the children of Israel shall a dog move its tongue, against man or beast, that you may know that the Lord does make a difference between the Egyptians and Israel" (Exodus 11:7).

This "difference" the Lord made between the Egyptians and His people should be of great encouragement to any of us who discover ourselves still on this planet longer than we anticipated!

God sent "destroying angels among them" (Psalm 78:49). Just as angels release plagues on earth in Rev. 16, angels were involved in the final plague of Egypt, the destruction of the firstborn. Israel was then given a mighty protection promise: "For the Lord will pass through to strike the Egyptians; and when He sees the blood on the lintel and on the two doorposts, the Lord will pass over the door and not allow the destroyer to come into your houses to strike you" (Ex. 12:23).

Anyone, anywhere, at any time...in ancient Egypt, in America today, or in a future time of angelic plagues...ANYONE who pleads the blood will not be destroyed by the destroyer. This would be a great time to sing that song *"When I see the blood, I will pass, I will pass over you."*

"Then the seventh angel poured out his bowl into the air, and a loud voice came out of the temple of heaven, from the throne, saying, "It is done!"" (Rev. 16:17). One day, God will at last say of the plagues and the wrath being poured out, "It is done!"

From the heavenly perspective, it is already a "done deal."

Chapter 17

Who Is the Harlot?

> "One of the 7 angels (said)…'Come, I will
> show you the judgment of the great harlot
> who sits on many waters'" (Rev. 17:1).

Chapter 17 is highly complex. The angel invites John to take a prophetic view of a future harlot (prostitute) in 17:1. This chapter is primarily written concerning that harlot (a metaphor).

Rev. 17:5 reveals her title: "**Mystery, Babylon the Great, the mother of harlots and of the abominations of the earth.**" A "Mystery" indeed! It's another hidden truth for us to "search out" (Prov. 25:2). This harlot has a name written on her forehead (**"Babylon the Great"**) which could either mean she in totality is THE Babylon (which we study in Chapter 18), or it could simply be saying she is an important part of Babylon (similar to a car revealing its ties to Detroit by having a sign written on it that says "Chevrolet").

17:1 says she **"sits on many waters"** (representing worldwide influence or even rulership!). 17:2 adds, "With whom the kings of the earth committed fornication." (World leaders "sleep" with her, another metaphor.) Further, "the inhabitants of the earth were made drunk with the wine of her fornication." Their "drunkenness" could represent their deception and confusion. Their "fornication" could be indicative of their unity or oneness with the harlot. Is this not what 1 Cor. 6:16 says: "**Do you know that he who is joined to a harlot is one body with her? For 'the two,' He says, shall become one flesh.**"

By now, you likely are thinking, *"Who is 'the great harlot'?"* For centuries, many Protestants believed the great harlot was none other than the Roman Catholic Church (headquartered in Rome). There seems to be evidence for this historically. And since Rome was in power at the time of John's writing, you can see why the Lord might not have allowed John to give a direct reference to Rome. To do so could have led to the persecution of Christians whose writings might have contained such treasonous ideas!

Through the centuries, many nations embraced Catholicism, and the Pope greatly influenced these nations. 17:18 gives a further clue: "**And the woman whom you saw is that great city which reigns over the kings of the earth.**" A "great city:" Rome? Or, as some now believe, Mecca? In the Islamic religion, "The Hajj" is an annual Muslim pilgrimage to Mecca, Saudi Arabia, the holiest city for Muslims, and all Muslims are encouraged to make the "Hajj" at least once in their life. And devout Muslims pray toward Mecca five times a day! Now THAT is an international influence!

Verse 17:9 mentions, "**The seven mountains on which the woman sits.**" It is a historical fact that Rome was built on seven hills! So that causes suspicion that the Catholic Church could be the harlot. However, personally, I don't believe that. Protestants share 32 cardinal doctrines with the Catholic Church. And Catholics are now a focal point for persecution around the world, along with Protestant Christians and Jews. That should say something! Meanwhile, don't let this mystery about the harlot bother you because an angel said: "**Come, I will show you**" (17:1).

Trust him to show you when you need to know.

His mysteries are on a need-to-know basis!

Fulfill His Purpose

> "For God has put it into their hearts to fulfill His purpose, to be of one mind, and to give their kingdom to the beast, until the words of God are fulfilled" (17:17).

The harlot "**was full of names of blasphemy**" (17:3). Protestants have long considered some of the doctrines of the Roman Catholic Church blasphemous or at least heretical: i.e. the selling of indulgences, the immaculate conception of Mary, papal infallibility (when he speaks doctrinally), prayers to saints and Mary, purgatory, etc.

Yet there are many priests, nuns, and other Catholics who are very godly. I am sure many will leave the Catholic Church if it heads south, just as many are leaving mainline Protestant churches as they have headed south! However (and I have believed this possibility for some time), the harlot could represent an apostate church of the end time—the "church" after the great falling away. This "church" would comprise the Roman Catholics, the Greek Orthodox Catholics, and Protestants alike, who have forsaken their first love.

Consider how many Protestants are now teaching blasphemous things: grace without works, no eternal hell, everybody will be saved, homosexual pastors and gay marriages allowed, etc.

Rev. 17:3 continues and speaks of the "**filthiness of her fornication.**" Christianity, long the leading champion of chastity, has now tragically and increasingly drifted away from that stance and tolerates or even encourages and invites sexual aberration among both members and the clergy. Many churches have members sitting in their pews who are sleeping together, unmarried (the most official definition of "fornication"). Surely the harlot could be the apostate "church."

One of the latest evolving theories is that Islam will be the religion the Antichrist uses to rise (and ride!) to power. Muslims represent over one-fourth (Where have we seen that figure before? Rev. 6:8) of the world, two plus billion people! And there are 50 nations with a Muslim majority! (Remember, in 17:1, the harlot sits on "many waters.")

Iran's Islamist leaders launched a satellite to help proclaim an end time theology. They believe the world must see chaos in order to bring back their Messiah, the Twelfth Imam! This certainly supports the theory of a Muslim Antichrist kingdom!

Religion, of some sort, will be a key feature of the Antichrist kingdom. Which religion he uses is conjecture, but that partnership will be a short-lived one: "**The beast will hate the harlot, make her desolate and naked, eat her flesh and burn her with fire**" (17:16). The nations loyal to the Antichrist (the 10 "horns" of v. 16) will turn on the harlot, whomever she represents, and destroy her. Why? Probably because the Antichrist plans to establish his own personal religion, with him being his own God! He does not want any competition!

Even in its carnal and lukewarm condition, the church is still a threat to him (because of the name of Jesus and the Word of God). Nevertheless, he will use religion in any way he can to advance his agenda. (This is like how political candidates can suddenly "find religion" to court voters!)

2 Thess. 2:4 speaks of this: "**The son of perdition...opposes and exalts himself above all that is called God or that is worshipped, so that he sits as God in the temple of God, showing himself that he**

is God." Wow! There's a rough road ahead for our planet! But, one verse should give us a little encouragement. **"God has put it into their hearts** (the nations that follow the beast) **to fulfill His purpose, to be of one mind, and to give their kingdom to the beast until the words of God are fulfilled"** (17:17).

If God can put world-changing things into the hearts of evil leaders, we should pray the Lord would "put it into the hearts" of our leaders to do what is right for America, Israel, other nations, and especially for the church. We desperately need Him to answer that prayer, now more than ever! I love the phrase: **"God has put."** God, not the Antichrist, has the ultimate say so in the Great Tribulation events! And I believe God will also **"put it into (our, His children's) hearts"** how to **"fulfill His purpose."** We will certainly need to also be "of one mind" to be most effective in this grand final conflict. But here is the part I especially like…

"**Until the words of God are fulfilled.**"

Every written word of God from the pages of the book of Revelation will be fulfilled!

GOD'S WORD WILL COME TO PASS…

…if not today, tomorrow, and if not tomorrow, by the time He arrives on this planet. Now do you see the importance of daily study of Revelation for your end times guidance? Hold on to all His Revelation promises! And make this your confession…

"I will 'fulfill His purpose'"

Chapter 18

Babylon the Great

> "Alas, alas, that great city Babylon,
> that mighty city! For in one hour your
> judgment has come" (Rev. 18:10).

For the Antichrist to rule the earth, he must control power worldwide in three areas:

1. **Political**, which always includes a Military (This was accomplished in Rev. 13)

2. **Religious** (We saw this accomplished in Rev. 17)

3. **Financial** (This is where I see chapter 18 coming in)

"Babylon the great is fallen, is fallen" (18:22). At first this might seem just a continuation of the judgment of the harlot (world religious systems) of chapter 17. But there seems to be a transition to the world financial system.

Money is necessary in today's world to "run" any religion. The Catholic Church, for instance, has an estimated worldwide financial value of 10 billion to two trillion! I am not going to criticize the

Catholic Church for this. It takes money to run ANY church! And it would be impossible for me, as a national evangelist, to continue this ministry without money (airfare, motels, rental cars, parking, food, etc.).

Politics and militaries help keep nations in partnership (e.g., NATO, Democracy, Communism). Religion gives nations a common interest, as in the Islamic world. Finances, however, are the one thing every person on earth has in common: we must have money to exist, or at least some medium of exchange, to even get our daily bread.

Babylon the Great, as I see it, is a picture of the financial systems of the world coming to a worldwide collapse. Remember, Babylon was the ancient area where the Tower of Babel was built. It was mankind's first attempt to try to "build a name for themselves" by building a tower that "reaches into the heavens" (Gen. 11:4).

Nimrod was, "the mighty hunter before the Lord" (Gen. 10:9). This is an expression thought to mean he was a hunter of men in defiance of the Lord. The historian Josephus suggests he was also the leader behind the building of the tower. But God confused their language, and Nimrod's grandiose ideas were thwarted!

Nimrod was, it seems, like the Antichrist, seeking to establish a political, religious, and financial kingdom. Later, other kings with far-reaching power would rule over this territory, still rebelling against God, in the "kingdom of Babylon." So, with that very brief history lesson, "Babylon" can symbolize any of men's confused attempts to reign on earth like a god!

Money is the one thing holding every "kingdom" together in a form of unity (i.e. China and the USA investing in one another, though religiously and politically at great odds, so both could mutually prosper financially). The world systems as they now exist must change dramatically for the Antichrist to rise to power. He'll need to control all buying and selling on earth (through the mark) and remove both communism and capitalism from its influence. Read 18:9-16 to see evidence for this interpretation of Babylon being a financial kingdom.

Then, 18:17 explains Babylon's fall: **"For in one hour, such great riches came to nothing. Every shipmaster, all who travel by ship, sailors, and as many as trade on the seas, stood at a distance and cried out when they saw the smoke of her burning, saying, 'What is like this great city?'"** I watched in astonishment the Twin Towers of New York City crumbling, 2001.9.11. I felt I was seeing the possible fulfillment of this prophecy. How could America ever recover from this estimated loss of up to two trillion dollars? Well, by God's grace, we came back from the brink, and the end wasn't yet. New York City fulfills the requirement of Babylon. It is the financial center of the earth!

Yet, "This great city" could also be simply metaphorical of the many, many cities around the globe with tall financial towers built to keep the world economy roaring. Or it could also represent some other city like Los Angeles. As I wrote earlier, Los Angeles is surely one of the most influential cities on earth, the premier center of entertainment (with Hollywood movies, Television studios, and Music production). I have long felt verses two and three sound like the global influence of Hollywood, just a few miles from downtown Los Angeles.

"Babylon the great has fallen…and has become a dwelling place of demons…for all the nations have drunk of the wine of the wrath of her fornication, the kings of the earth have committed fornication with her" (18:2, 3). Ninety percent of the pornography on earth is produced in "Porn Valley" (San Fernando Valley) just outside of Hollywood! If ever a city was **"a dwelling place of demons,"** surely Los Angeles could qualify!

Consider also 18:21, 2: **"The great city Babylon shall be thrown down and shall not be found anymore. The sound of…musicians…**

shall not be heard in you anymore." Hollywood's evil influence (through its music, TV, and movies) is utterly dependent on people having money to go to concerts and theaters, pay for TV cable, or pay for physical performances or records or now, streaming, and that's without mentioning the cost of advertising!

Think how the entertainment industry would collapse overnight if suddenly people could no longer afford to go to theaters or keep up with their cable TV bills, cell phones, etc. I wonder about the young people who listen to music by the hour when their plug is pulled "in one hour." As I ride on jets to my meetings, people sit next to me and almost immediately put their earphones in and start listening to their music or watching videos.

God got the world's attention as we watched the Twin Towers in New York crumble before our eyes. But Americans built a new tower, and New York recovered. But one day, likely very soon: "**The great city Babylon shall be thrown down and shall not be found anymore.**" Don't trust Wall Street. Don't trust the impressive towers in NY, LA, or your state's biggest city. We will one day be delivered from all "**dwelling places of demons.**" Babylon, after centuries of contending for earthly control, will finally fall forever.

Rejoice at Babylon's Fall

> "Your merchants were the great men
> of the earth, for by your sorcery all the
> nations were deceived" (Rev. 18:23).

Sorcery is used to effect change by magical means. Money is certainly "magical," isn't it? "**The love of money is the root of all evil**" (1 Tim. 6:10 KJV). Money buys sex and it buys political favors; it also buys military weapons. Tragically, it has also bought many Christians, including preachers. (One preacher I read about was being indicted for absconding with $500,000 of the church's funds. He apparently committed suicide!).

Rev. 18:24 ends the chapter with, "In her (Babylon) **was found the blood of prophets and saints, and of all who were slain on the earth.**" Think about it! Political power, military power, religious power, and financial power—at least one of these features of Babylon the Great was behind all martyrdom throughout history!

"**Therefore, her plagues will come in one day—death and mourning and famine. And she will be utterly burned with fire, for strong is the Lord God who judges her**" (18:8). This isn't the work of the Antichrist, but the hand of God! A terrible earthquake in Los Angeles or a suitcase-size atomic bomb detonated in lower Manhattan, New York, could certainly be all it would take to start a free-fall of the entire world economy.

The fall of Babylon could occur concurrently with the seals or the woes of the angels in earlier chapters. Do not take for granted that it happens after the rapture because of the warning in 18:4: "**Come out of her, my people, lest you share in her sins, and lest you receive of her plagues.**" *You can't come out of something you aren't already in, so prepare to possibly be here to see this coming fall of Babylon!*

Prepare to "come out" of what is brewing into a pit of judgment as noted in 18:4.

COME OUT of all "habitations of demons."

COME OUT of churches where they are falling by the sorcery of false religion.

COME OUT of a political system that is headed toward oneness with the Antichrist. Beware of any political party that believes in murdering babies. This is what Herod did when he felt his political power was threatened by Jesus. Beware of any party that champions any and all sexual rights. And beware of any party that endangers freedom of speech or religion!

COME OUT of a future financial system where you can only buy or sell if you take the mark.

Yet, we can rejoice in the glorious results from Babylon's fall.

1. Politically, we will be "avenged" as we will begin to rule and reign with Christ for a thousand years on earth!

2. Militarily, we will be "avenged" as we "overcome (Satan) by the blood of the lamb" (12:11).

3. Religiously, we will be "avenged" when, at last, every other world religion realizes CHRIST REALLY WAS THE ONLY WAY TO GOD! And finally,

4. Financially, as we walk with streets made of gold as heirs of God and joint-heirs of Christ.

To me, the keyword in the entire chapter 18 for believers is simply (And we should be doing this all the time anyway)...

"**Rejoice over her, O heaven, and you holy apostles and prophets, for God, has avenged you on her**" (18:20). REJOICE is the keyword! If you end up having to be here for some of this, you intend to COME OUT, don't you? Then, you are promised that your vengeance is coming! So...

Rejoice!

Chapter 19

The Bride of Christ

"The marriage of the Lamb has come, and His wife has made herself ready" (19:7).

The belief in a rapture before the events of chapters 5-18 must be called into question because in the verse above, we are told, "the marriage of the Lamb has come." This, at the very least, shows we must not read Revelation sequentially, and at the most, is evidence of a rapture, not before, but during the Great Tribulation.

Also, Bible scholars disagree as to whether this "marriage" includes a supper beginning immediately after a pretribulation rapture, a midtribulation, or post. Some think the "marriage" takes place in heaven, but the "supper" may not be celebrated until the millennium begins.

"His wife has made herself ready. And to her it was granted to be arrayed in fine linen, clean and bright, for the fine linen is the righteous acts of the saints" (19:7, 8). Two CERTAIN things are said, however, about the church now gathered in heaven…

1. The bride of Christ had "made itself ready." Notice it doesn't

say: "The Lord cleaned them all up, by His grace, and they are unworthy to be here, yet they nevertheless made it in." Do you think maybe obeying and overcoming are involved in truly being the end time bride of Christ?

2. She was "arrayed in fine linen...for the fine linen is the righteous acts of the saints." Why didn't it say they were saved by grace and acts were irrelevant? The Blood that washes our garments and makes them white as snow is the same Blood that helps us overcome and live with righteous "acts." I hope preachers make this clear to the end times church! Revelation clearly gives us guidance to do more than just believe!

Paul was the world's champion preacher of grace, yet he warned: **"Wherefore, my beloved, as ye have always obeyed, not as in my presence only, but now much more in my absence, WORK OUT your own salvation with fear and trembling. For it is God which worketh in you both to will and to do of his good pleasure" (Phil. 2:12, 13 KJV). It says "work out."** We "work out" what God has already "worked in us." Salvation and walking in faith with obedience to Christ, results in "righteous acts." It is not salvation by works, but a salvation that ALWAYS has attendant works! Good works and righteous acts: It's what His saints always have and always should and must do. Let this be your confession now and in any future tribulations you may face...

"I believe; therefore, I do righteous acts."

Your Prophecy

"The testimony of Jesus is the spirit of prophecy" (Rev. 19:10).

Every time we testify about the Lord, the Holy Spirit is using our mouths, in a sense, to prophesy to people. "**The Spirit of truth (The Holy Spirit)...will testify of me**" (John 15:26). The Prophet John the Baptist, "**bore witness to the truth**" (John 5:33). Jesus is "**the Way the Truth and the Life**" (John 14:6). The truth Jesus taught is something we must be diligent to bear witness of. And such witness is "**the spirit of prophecy.**"

Prophesy to sinners often! Jesus said: "**If you forgive the sins of any, they are forgiven them; if you retain the sins of any, they are retained**" (John 20:23). Thus, from the mouth of our Lord, we have a commission and a legal authority to, like prophets, proclaim to the lost...

"If you repent and turn to Christ, your sins will be forgiven, and you will make heaven your home, but if you don't repent and turn to Christ, you will die in your sins and end up in hell."

Christians have an awesome privilege and responsibility as "prophets" to this world!

There is another application of Rev. 19:10. God uses some in the gift of prophecy (the actual gift akin to Old Testament prophets; Ssee 1 Cor. 12:10, 14:5, 24, 25). Concerning this gift, Paul wrote: "**You may all prophesy**" (1 Cor. 14:31). When the gift of prophecy (which can include the gift of the word of knowledge, word of wisdom, or discerning of spirits) is manifested by prophesying, the "testimony of Jesus" is given. In other words, when one prophesies by the inspiration of the Holy Spirit, He professes: This is what Jesus is saying at this time about this situation."

Prophecy is a greatly needed gift for today's confused world! Moses exclaimed in Numbers 11:29, "Oh, that all the Lord's people were prophets and that the Lord would put His Spirit upon them." The gift of prophecy is promised to the last-day generation: "And it shall come to pass in the last days, says God, That I will pour out of My Spirit on all flesh; YOUR SONS AND YOUR DAUGHTERS SHALL PROPHESY" (Acts 2:17). I have prayed that verse over my children and grandchildren many times. In my jogs, I often pass an elementary school and pray that verse over the children and on students at a college campus!

In this desperate hour, may the testimony of Jesus, the spirit of prophecy, abide on us all, especially our children and grandchildren! Let us endeavor to be prophets. Prophesy, especially by sharing the testimony that Jesus is alive and coming soon! When you witness to the unsaved, you are as mighty as the prophets Isaiah or Jeremiah! When you share the gospel with a sinner, you are like an anointed Old Testament prophet to them! Heaven or hell...

Your testimony prophesies an eternal destiny for sinners!

The Lord of War

> "Then I saw heaven opened, and behold, a white horse. And He who sat on him was called Faithful and True, and in righteousness He judge and makes war" (19:11).

In the Old Testament, the phrase "The Lord of hosts (or armies)" was the most often used title for the Lord. In chapter 19, the Lord returns to earth. Many call this His Second Coming. But before He "judges," He must first "make war." The battle of Armageddon is fought at this time...

"I saw the beast, the kings of the earth, and their armies, gathered together to make war against Him who sat on the horse and against His army. Then the beast was captured, and with him the false prophet who worked signs in his presence, by which he deceived those who received the mark of the beast and those who worshiped his image. These two were cast alive into the lake of fire… And the rest were killed with the sword which proceeded from the mouth of Him who sat on the horse" (19:29-21).

Thus, the Great Tribulation comes to an end. Hallelujah!

Happy Days are here again!

Chapter 20

Satan Bound

"He (an angel) laid hold of the dragon, that serpent of old, who is the Devil and Satan, and bound him for a thousand years" (20:1).

The angel "cast him into the bottomless pit" (20:2). The "bottomless pit" is a translation of two Greek Words…

1. "avyssos" which means "without" and…

2. "byssos" which means "depth or bottom."

And he will be chained there for 1000 years. How wonderful the earth will be after that happens.

Beheaded

"I saw the souls of them who had been beheaded for their witness to Jesus and for the word of God" (Rev. 20:4).

Many Christians could die as martyrs in the end times. There were probably hundreds of millions of Christians gathered around the throne of God who had died natural deaths or had been raptured into heaven, but this verse only gives mention of one special group: **"the souls of those who had been beheaded."**

We know Christians are persecuted and martyred for their faith in Christ. But notice that they were **"beheaded...*FOR THE WORD OF GOD.*"** It is one thing to say, *"I refuse to take the mark because I refuse to renounce Christ."* But why would it say, **"for the word of God?"** Paul warned: **"In the latter times, some will depart from the faith, giving heed to deceiving spirits and doctrines of demons"** (1 Tim. 4:1). False teachings, teachings inspired by demons, and doctrines so heretical they will cause many to **"depart from the faith"** will arise in the **"latter times."** What are some of these teachings? 1 Tim. 4:3 says at least two of these doctrines of demons will be...

1. **"forbidding to marry"**

What is marriage but a covenantal God-ordained relationship between a man and a woman? Those who think their "love" or intention to marry in the future, or those who are in a sexual bond apart from a wedding ring, have in essence yielded to doctrines of demons who have forbidden them from marrying. Some move in together for financial reasons: **"the love of money is the root of all evil (evils like fornication!)."** (1 Tim. 6:10).

2. **"Commanding to abstain from foods."**

Could veganism or the "save the earth by not eating beef" concept be possible forerunners of coming doctrines or "laws" that control what we are allowed to eat? Or even FDA regulations for our "health?"

Christians will, under the Antichrist rule, become martyrs, beheaded: **"for the word of God."** Many are making choices, even now, to reject the clear-cut teachings of the Bible by accepting the doctrines of demons. Their choices may save their life for a while, as they will not be a threat to the antichrist, but those unbiblical choices could tragically cause them to continue their slide into ever more devilish doctrines until they, at last, succumb to the worst doctrinal deception of all time, which is to:

Worship the antichrist and receive his mark!

Some false doctrines are relatively petty and hinder effective Christian living. But some are evil and demonic in their origin. A few of these doctrines will, as Paul warned in Timothy 4:1, even cause people to **"depart from the faith."** (Isn't this speaking about Christians? You can't depart from a place where you haven't already been. These were "in the faith" and were deceived into leaving it!).

The Word of God is the foundation of the faith: **"Faith comes by hearing…the Word of God"** (Romans 10:17). Thus, as His children, we must hold fast to the "doctrine of Christ" as the Bible teaches and choose the truth of the Word of God even if this decision may one day cost us our lives! 2 John 7-11 pictures this clearly: **"For many deceivers have gone out into the world who do not confess Jesus Christ as coming in the flesh. This is a deceiver and an antichrist. Look to yourselves…Whoever transgresses and does not abide in the doctrine of Christ does not have God. He who abides in the doctrine of Christ has both the Father and the Son. If anyone comes to you and does not bring this doctrine, do not receive him into your house nor greet him; for he who greets him shares in his evil deeds."**

Does that sound like letting anyone and everyone join our churches and not be so dogmatic and judgmental? No, just the opposite! The day will come when Christians must take a stand for the "doctrine" of the Word of God and not receive "the antichrist" deceivers into our homes or churches or share in the evil deeds of those who are falling away!

To those reading this who may one day become a martyr, receive hope and inspiration from this fact: *God Himself puts a special eternal value upon the souls of those who face martyrdom for His sake*: **"Then I saw the souls of those who had been beheaded for their witness to Jesus"** (20:4). Many others were saved and in heaven at the time of this revelation. Why would John especially mention martyrs? Probably for the same reason Jesus stood to His feet from His position seated next to the Father, as the first martyr, Stephen was preparing to enter heaven (Acts 8). Jesus was proud of His Martyr and wanted to give Stephen the honor due to him! "Those who honor me, them will I honor" (1 Sam. 2:30).

Martyrs are very special people to God! (After all, they truly "shared in Christ's sufferings" in the most real sense!). God called Moses "**My servant.**" He called Abraham His "**friend.**" What wonderful Characterizations! Yet there is one title, in my opinion, which is the greatest of them all! It's the title given to one of the early martyrs of the church in Rev. 2:13: "**Antipas…my faithful martyr.**"

I feel that I will likely one day be a martyr. To be honest, I would rather be 8,276 rows back from Christ's throne among the many millions of others who were raptured to heaven. But what consolation: one day, I might instead be sitting on the third row from the throne throughout eternity (like when I sat on the third row at a Christmas play to proudly watch my 7-year-old grandson sing in the children's school choir!).

And just imagine, my precious Lord, might proudly refer to me as "**Dea Warford, My faithful martyr.**" So, just in case it comes to it, may I encourage you to sign your name in the blank space below…

(_____) "**My faithful martyr.**"

That dramatically changes the whole perspective of end times persecution, doesn't it?

The Book of Life

"And whosoever was not found written in the book of life was cast into the lake of fire" (Rev. 20:15).

The Book of Life is the second most important book in the universe after the Bible. It determines who spends eternity in heaven and who spends eternity in hell. Read the whole context of this verse...

"And the devil that deceived them was cast into the lake of fire and brimstone, where the beast and the false prophet are, and shall be tormented day and night forever and ever. And I saw a great white throne, and Him that sat on it, from whose face the earth and the heaven fled away; and there was found no place for them. And I saw the dead, small and great, stand before God; and the books were opened: and another book was opened, which is the book of life: and the dead were judged out of those things which were written in the books, according to their works. And the sea gave up the dead which were in it; and death and hell delivered up the dead which were in them: and they were judged every man according to their works. And death and hell were cast into the lake of fire. This is the second death. And whosoever was not found written in the book of life was cast into the lake of fire" (Rev. 20:10-15).

I wrote a lot about hell in my book *ABOUT THE FUTURE* if you want to study hell further. Hell is one of my deepest personal concerns. During a church service where I was ministering, I asked everyone in the congregation to raise their hand, explaining: *"If God gave you the choice of going to heaven for five minutes to see what it is like or going to hell for five minutes, which would you prefer?"*

First, I asked for the hands of those who would rather go to heaven for five minutes. *EVERYBODY RAISED THEIR HAND!*

Then I asked how many would prefer to visit hell. Not one raised a hand, but I did!

I WAS THE ONLY ONE TO RAISE MY HAND!

Why was that so? As an evangelist, I have a very special calling to help men, women, and children to escape an eternity in hell! For this reason, I think about death and hell often. I somehow feel if the Lord would take me to hell for just five minutes, and I could see with my own eyes (not just by faith) its horrors, maybe I would witness, pray, and work harder and thus help even more souls escape this tragic future.

The Lord has shown others hell, and they always give the most awful descriptions. Most of us must accept the fires of hell by faith by what God's word says about it: "**But the cowardly, unbelieving, abominable murderers, sexually immoral, sorcerers, idolaters, and all liars shall have their part in the lake which burns with fire and brimstone, which is the second death**" (21:8).

Some mistakenly think the phrase "the second death" means a quick, final destruction that destroys both soul and body. Rightly dividing the word, and as a second witness, Rev. 14:10 says all who take the mark of the beast "**shall be tormented with fire and brimstone… And the smoke of their torment ascends forever and ever, and they have no rest day or night.**"

People report the death of an unsaved person often by saying, *"They died peacefully in their sleep surrounded by loved ones."* What difference does it make if they died peacefully or in terrible pain while begging for morphine? Immediately after their death, without Christ, they go straight to an eternal, painful hell! No unsaved person will ever "rest in peace." Eternal punishment is one of our greatest motivators for evangelism.

Yet, thank God, if you are a Christian, there is a "book of life" with your name in it! It is your ticket to heaven and your "get out of hell free card!" 20:12 mentions "books" that record our works from which we will be judged: the righteous, to determine their eternal rewards; and the unsaved, to determine the severity of their eternal punishments. I memorized verses 20:11-15 when I was a teenager. Its truth has flavored my life, as it should us all! I believe it is very important we have a full understanding of the significance of the book of life.

Another insight is 20:12: "**the books were opened: and another book was opened, which is the book of life: and the dead were judged out of those things which were written in the books, according to their works.**" Each person is writing his own eternal autobiography filled with the words, deeds, and thoughts of a lifetime. Perhaps our personal angel is recording it all in the books mentioned above. But you can be sure the whole book will be read at the judgment, except for our sins, which have been unrecorded and completely forgotten: "**Their sins and their iniquities I will remember no more**" (Heb. 8:12). Is your autobiography a good book, with no need of much heavenly editing?

The Bible says a lot more about this book of life. Following the scriptural interpretation of "law of first mention," we first read of the book in Exodus 32:31-33 where Moses prays, "**Oh, these people have committed a great sin, and have made for themselves a god of gold! Yet now, if You will forgive their sin—but if not, I pray, blot me out of Your book which You have written**" (God replied to Moses) "**Whoever has sinned against Me, I will blot him out of My book.**"

This is obviously referring to the book of life! Notice God says it is "My book." He created it and writes or blots out names from that book at His own discretion. That Moses was willing to have his name removed from that book for the sake of others reveals why God chose him in the first place: Moses was the greatest intercessor of all time.

Would to God lost sinners had someone with that love and devotion to intercede on their behalf! Is that one you?

Also note, **"Whoever (Moses, you, me!) has sinned against Me, I will blot him out of my book."** Sin is the primary reason names are removed from that book! Preachers who preach love, faith, grace, and prosperity better note this truth carefully! A pastor of a church where I preached reported that I *"gave a passionate plea for the unsaved to give their lives to Christ." A "passionate plea"* should be every Christian's appeal to the lost because of their eternally damning sin! Is it your plea?

Who was the first person to have their name written in the book of life? I suggest Abel! **"By faith Abel offered unto God a more excellent sacrifice than Cain, by which he obtained witness that he was righteous, God testifying of his gifts and by it he being dead yet speaks"** (Heb. 11:4). If God lists names in the book of life according to when one dies, Abel's name was first in that book. What an honor!

Ps. 87:5, 6: **"And of Zion (God's people!) It shall be said, "This and that man was born in her and the highest himself shall establish her. The Lord shall count, when he writes up the people (in the book of life?) that this man was born there."** When does the Lord "write up the people" and our names are written in the book of life? **"The beast...shall ascend out of the bottomless pit, and go into perdition: and they...on the earth shall wonder, whose names were not written in the book of life from the foundation of the world"** (Rev. 17:8).

At the beginning of time, the Lord prepared the book of life and wrote names in that book. Some believe God wrote everybody's name who would ever live throughout history, revealing His love and that **"He desires all men to be saved and to come to the knowledge of the truth"** (1 Tim. 2:4). Then, sadly, by their own choices in life, most names one by one are blotted out, perhaps not until the moment of their death, when all opportunities for them ever to be saved are finally exhausted.

Others believe God, in His foreknowledge, wrote down the names of all who would one day be born again. They need only keep their name there by enduring to the end. Then, there is a unique group of people mentioned in Rev. 13:8: "**And all that dwell upon the earth shall worship him (the beast) whose names are not written in the book of life.**" In the end times, all who receive the mark of the beast have their names blotted out (likely at that moment of decision), so their names are no longer written in that book, this is if they ever were. In the fear of God, carefully guard yourself against the deception of sin so your name is never blotted out of His book!

Names Written in Heaven

"Don't rejoice that spirits are subject to you; but rather rejoice, because your names are written in heaven" (Luke 10:20).

There are places in the scripture where it doesn't say "book of life," but we can infer from the context it refers to that book: "**and at that time (at the close of this age) your people shall be delivered, every one that shall be found written in the book.**" God's people will be delivered from the Great Tribulation, but ONLY those "**found written in the book.**"

Because of the "great falling away" and horrific trials of that time, many will have their name blotted out of the book of life. Jesus warned us: "**he who endures to the end, shall be saved**" (Mark 13:13). Hard times are coming! Zealously guard your name's position in that book! Endure temptation, allurements to sin, and persecution. Endure to the end!

Another probable mention of the Book of Life is in Malachi 3:16, 17: "Then they that feared the Lord spoke often to one another" (We need to speak to one another more! In. Heb. 10:25, the Lord warns against the folly of forsaking the fellowship of the saints in end times) "and the Lord hearkened, and heard it." He heard what? Our encouraging words to one other, our confession of His promises, and our prayers of agreement.

Malachi continues, "and a book of remembrance was written before Him for them that feared the Lord" (I believe the book of remembrance is the book of life!) "And they shall be mine." The word "mine" is fraught with truth.

Decades ago, an infant child had been taken from a drug-addicted relative. We were searching for someone to adopt her. A childless Christian couple came to my office to meet me and discuss it. My family members and I approved of them, and they adopted her. After the adoption was final, the new mother joyfully told me, *"She's all mine!"* In other words, no more visitations from unstable parents, snoopy eyes from a suspicious relative, and no intrusions by the government. The little girl had a mother and a father. Hallelujah! One day, the Lord will boast of us, *"They're all Mine!"* No more visitations from the devil, no more judgmental eyes from the world, no more separation from the Father forever and ever.

Then Malachi continues, "in that day when I make up my jewels" (The Lord intends to make us like high-quality, shining jewelry treasured and worn close to His heart forever!) and I will spare them, as a man spares his own son that serves him."

Jesus surely referred to the book of life: "Don't rejoice that spirits are subject to you; but rather rejoice, because your names are written in heaven" (Luke 10:20). I cast a demon out for the first time in May 1976 while pastoring in Walla Walla, WA. I was so thrilled afterward that I was speeding home to tell my wife about it. A cop had to pull me over for breaking the law! There's nothing on earth quite like confronting an alien from hell and vanquishing it! Yet, Jesus said having your name written in heaven far exceeds even the most amazing earthly experiences.

You know demons are subject to you. Is your name "written" in heaven? If so, you can... **Rejoice!**

Most Important Registration

Paul refers to that book in Philippians 4:3: "help those women which labored with me in the gospel...and the rest of my fellow workers, whose names are written in the Book of Life."

The most important thing you could ever say about anybody is that their "**names are written in the Book of Life.**" Can you say that about yourself? Can your workmates? One million years from today, nobody will be walking around saying, *"My name was written on the registration of my shiny new Ford."* More likely, we will often hear,

"I'm so thankful my name was written in heaven."

"You are come unto Mount Zion unto the city of the living God, the heavenly Jerusalem, and to an innumerable company of angels, To the general assembly and church of the firstborn, which are written in heaven" (Hebrews 12:22, 23). It is "the general assembly" and the "church" whose "names are written in heaven." As a personal evangelist, when someone tells me they do not attend church, to me, that's usually a sign their name is probably NOT written in heaven!

What a privilege to have our names in the book of life! And just think, it's all because of Jesus! "And there shall in no wise enter into it (the New Jerusalem) **anything that defiles, neither whoever works abomination, or makes a lie: but they which are written in the Lamb's Book of Life**" (21:27). The book belongs to the Lamb, Jesus. His sacrifice gave us the right to be written in that book. It is "the Lamb's".

Rev. 13:8 says more about the Lamb: "And all that dwell upon the earth shall worship him (the beast) whose names are not written in the book of life of the Lamb slain from the foundation of the world." Can you envision a scene in heaven, as I do, at "the foundation of the world," of Jesus appearing before the Father when the Son offers to become a "Lamb slain" for the future race of mankind? Every angel was invited to this glorious event. They sing and stand in awe as the Father hands Jesus a book. Did Jesus take time (remember, it is eternity) to read each name one by one? Did He read your name? Did He read mine? And after the full realization of the eternal worth of our souls, the Godhead had a conversation: "Whom shall I send, and who will go for us. Then said I, 'Here am I; send me'" (Isa. 6:8).

Jesus said, "I will!" Then He left heaven to become a sacrificial Lamb: "When He came into the world, He said, "Sacrifice and offering you desired not, but a body you have prepared for me ... Then said I, Look, I come (in the volume of the book it is written of me) to do Your will, O God" (Heb. 10:5-7). Jesus alone deserves our passionate service! Those who reject the greatest love the world has ever known will themselves be rejected on that day. It's all recorded in a book!

No wonder Jesus said: "Whoever shall be ashamed of me and of my words in this sinful generation; of him also shall the Son of man be ashamed when He comes in the glory of His Father with the angels" (Mark 8:38). Do you witness for Christ in public and stand up for your faith?

In view of all these sobering truths, may I ask again: Are you giving a "passionate plea for the unsaved to give their lives to Christ?" If not, begin doing so. In fact, a good way to begin such a witness would be to ask:

"Is your name written in the Book of Life?"

1,000 Years on Earth

> "Blessed and holy is he who has part in the
> first resurrection. Over such the second
> death has no power, but they shall be priests
> of God and of Christ, and shall reign with
> Him a thousand years" (Rev. 20:6).

I have never heard a sermon on the Millennium. In fact, I doubt many Christians have even given it much thought. Have you? I couldn't even find a book on that subject in an Amazon search! Yet, the Bible says much about this 10-century future period of human history.

We will spend a short time in heaven after the rapture, maybe three to seven years, depending on your beliefs, but it could be just a matter of days! We will then return to the earth to live here for a thousand years (Rev. 20:4). It will still be our present earth, but there will be big changes!

Satan is "cast into the bottomless pit" so he can no longer deceive people (Rev. 20:3). This will significantly reduce evil during this period. The Bible doesn't mention demons during the Millennium. They could be bound away with Satan or still allowed to roam the Earth. But that would just give us more fun things to do, like casting demons out!

Jesus will set up His "headquarters" in Jerusalem (Zech. 14:16, 17). And the redeemed "shall reign with Him a thousand years." This Millennial reign of Christ excites me for a lot of reasons. Consider: "the Lord shall be King over all the earth" (Zech. 14:9); And He "shall rule them with a rod of iron" (Rev. 2:27). The most exciting thing is, we get to rule with Him! "The time came that the saints possessed the kingdom" and "the kingdom and dominion, and *the greatness of the kingdom under the whole heaven, shall be given to* … the saints of the Most High, whose kingdom is an everlasting kingdom, and all dominions shall serve and obey him" (Dan. 7:22, 25).

I often revel in this coming privilege! As I've prayed, "**For thine is the kingdom,**" I've oft thanked the Lord I will be a part of this coming kingdom! Neither Hollywood nor Washington will any longer be earth's most influential city. In this kingdom, Jerusalem will be the very center of the universe! All nations will journey there at least once a year to worship Him (Zech. 14:16, 17). Many make it a big deal to go to the Holy Land and see all the sites. That isn't important to me. Why? Because during the Millennium, I'll visit the Holy Land at least 1000 times! Why spend hard-earned cash now to see sites that are reputed to be the place where events took place when actual Bible characters that lived there can show us the actual sites and relate to us personally how things really went down?

What will life be like during the Millennium? "**The creature itself also shall be delivered from the bondage of corruption into the glorious liberty of the children of God**" (Rom. 8:21 KJV). The planet, the people, and even animals will all experience the benefit of the church manifested to the full measure of its glorious destiny!

There will be many unsaved men and women who "happened" to survive the horrors of the Great Tribulation. We don't know how many, but we do know over half the population of Earth is gone! There will still be billions left! Billions for believers to help "rule over." What will our rulership entail? We'll likely be Governors, Senators, Mayors, Chiefs of Police, college regents, and school principals. And there will be a great need for pastors, teachers, and missionaries to lead the nations in the ways of the Lord. "**The earth shall be full of the knowledge of the Lord as the waters cover the sea**" (Isa. 11:9). Oh, what joy to lead people to Christ with righteous knowledge covering the entire earth! Churches, auditoriums, and stadiums will be filled! Imagine the revival taking place worldwide!

I believe this will especially be true of the Muslim World: **"Then the Lord will be known to Egypt, and the Egyptians will know the Lord in that day... Israel will be one of three with Egypt and Assyria"** (Isa. 19:18-25). Murderers will be quickly executed when the Lord rules with His "rod of iron!" Crime will be significantly minimized! (No more "no-bail" release to the streets!). And even terrorists will come to Christ!

The tribulation judgments, which will have destroyed much of the earth, will be but the terminal reaping of what was sown by Adam in the fall of man. However, many of the effects of sin will be reversed during the Millennium. The Lord could do this instantly with a wave of His hand. But just as He allowed angels to do many things on His behalf, He'll allow us the privilege of doing the same.

One of the first things we'll likely need to do after our return is to start the restoration process for this planet. There will be a big mess after seven years of judgment! Five earthquakes are mentioned in Revelation: 6:12, 8:5, 11:13; 11:19; (the last, 16:18, 19, being the greatest of all time): **"There was a great earthquake, such as was not since men were upon the earth, so mighty an earthquake, and so great. And the great city was divided into three parts, and the cities of the nations fell."** We'll need major citywide construction projects, necessitating engineers and laborers to literally rebuild the cities of the earth. The church will surely lead this historic building project (second only to the Tower of Babel).

There is no unemployment problem during the Millennium. Likely many of us will use skills we picked up in our lifetime and continue in our same career (But no longer the guy on the bottom digging the ditch, instead, up on top giving orders!). Others could enroll in a university to study for the career they've always wanted. Doctor? Become one! Maybe I'll be your teacher if you want to be an evangelist! Or, I'll sit down in the class with you while an angel teaches us both! However, there is no mention of what angels do during the Millennium, so they may still remain usually invisible in the background while we visibly work in the foreground!

I personally believe one purpose of the 1,000 years is to even things up a bit. God is a fair God! Many women would have loved to have children but couldn't or lost theirs. No problem: they will have their own preschool and nursery and raise children like their own family! Neglected Down Syndromes? They'll be Ph.D. professors! Low-paid LVN nurses will be chief surgeons in hospitals. A hard life of poverty for 80 years? Faithful saints will be squatters in unoccupied Beverly Hills mansions for 1000 years! Remember two thrilling coming events:

We live on Earth for 1000 years!

We reign over billions of people for 1000 years!

Reign With Christ

"And they lived and reigned with Christ for a thousand years" (20:4). Yes, living and reigning on earth for a thousand years is a wonderful thought! But note that we "**reign with Christ.**" He will be the very best thing about those 1000 years!

"The wolf also shall dwell with the lamb ...and a little child shall lead them. And the cow and the bear shall feed; their young ones shall lie down together: and the lion shall eat straw like the ox. And the sucking child shall play on the hole of the asp, and the weaned child shall put his hand in the viper's den. They shall not hurt nor destroy in all my holy mountain" (Isa. 11:6-9). Life on earth will become fantastic! The verse above reveals some remarkable differences. Animals began killing and eating one another after the fall, but during the Millennium, it appears all animals will be vegetarians. (Maybe mankind will be, too! I assure you, if so, they will have some fantastic veggie burgers available by then!)

Since one-third of the trees and grass are burned up (Rev. 8:7), there will likely be a massive agricultural revolution to restore the earth to its pre-fall Garden of Eden-like splendor. (You farmers and all those who love gardening will have a ball!) And watch how we totally eradicate weeds!

Verse 9:8 speaks of a "great mountain burning with fire." A comet or meteor will destroy one-third of sea life. That event will require quite an ecological strategy to restore the ocean, clean up shorelines, and rebuild coastal communities. A hard job, but in our glorified bodies, all work will be fun and exciting, like it must have been for Adam before the curse.

Peek into the Millennium: **"There will no longer be an infant who lives for only a few days or an old man who doesn't live a long life. Whoever lives to be a hundred years old will be thought of as young. Whoever dies before he is a hundred years old will be cursed as a sinner"** (Isa. 65:20 GW). Childhood diseases could be eradicated. Medical and health advancements will make living over 100 years of age easy to reach. Many of us could be "miracle workers" stationed at hospitals, ready to pray for "stillborn" infants or dying patients. Others ride in ambulances, ready to heal the sick or wounded, or even raise the dead!

Isaiah mentions death. Though we, the redeemed, will be in our glorified bodies and never again experience death, the earth will be populated by people who will die. Hopefully, most of the unsaved left on earth (or born during the thousand years) will submit to the gospel and be ready to face eternity. Yet, many will reject the gospel, even in the face of Christ's rulership and love on display! Some will die by disease, murder, or accidents, though such things will be minimized by our glorified leadership, oversight, and "witty inventions" to restore earth.

Nevertheless, as a form of judgment because of their stubborn sin or unbelief, early death will come to those whom, as Isaiah predicts above, will be considered **"cursed as a sinner."** Further proof that many will remain unsaved in spite of our best efforts is revealed in Rev. 20:1, 2, 7-9: After 1000 years, Satan will be unleashed from his chain in his prison chains and once more deceive a **"number as the sand of the sea"** (20:8). Their rebellion, thankfully, is short-lived and unsuccessful. God never has and never will make people love Him, even during the Millennium!

What fabulous rewards await the righteous! We'll have a thousand years to see everything we ever wanted to see and do everything we ever wanted to do. Like Philip, we may be able to fly or quickly move from one location to another. Since we won't have to sleep, maybe we'll have wonderful fellowship services or parties every night! *Before we leave this old earth behind, let's have a long, glorious farewell ceremony!*

Some may feel a certain sadness at the thought of ever having to say goodbye to this planet. But learn something from my experience. I have preached in all 50 states. I have flown into most major cities. I have seen most of the great tourist sites of our nation. I've climbed the Empire State Building, ridden on the Gateway Arch across the Mississippi, felt the mist at Niagara Falls, seen the stately Newport Mansions in Rhode Island, been to Disneyworld, walked the River Walk in San Antonio, TX, strolled through the Smithsonian Museums in Washington D.C. and on and on.

I have seen so much of America after seven decades that now, when I go to a city for a crusade, I rarely take time to see any of the sites. I go from the airport to the motel, to the restaurant, to the gym, to the church, and repeat again and again until I fly back home. If traveling for a career for only decades has sated my need to see much else in America, imagine after you have had 1000 years to explore your planet! Don't you think you will be ready for the new heavens and new earth by then? I'm sure you will.

For many of us (certainly for me), it is hard to imagine what heaven is like. So we can find comfort in the truth that we will be right here on terra firma, home sweet home, for longer than we can imagine before we finally say adieu! For many years now, I have often tried to imagine how long 1000 years is. When I was 50, I probably thought to myself: *"Wow, I have had a lot of experiences and seen so many things. But, I can look forward to 20 times as many years to enjoy the Millennium."* At nearly 75 now, that period is about 13 times as long! I feel I have lived a fabulous life! Still, I genuinely look forward to over 365,000 days of enjoying the Lord's presence on earth with His church promoted to all its destined splendor and glory! I'll visit Africa and see the lions! I'll fly to Saturn and see what the rings look like. I'll preach the gospel with joy and power like never before. This incredible time is just ahead of you, too. Yet, first, the greatest trial the world has ever known must take place. When it does, and if you are still here, don't fall away! Keep the faith! Because then, for a thousand years, you get to...

Reign with Christ!

Chapter 21

The New Earth

"I saw a new heaven and a new earth,
for the first heaven and the first earth
had passed away" (Rev. 21:1).

(You may be surprised at this comment: *After the new earth becomes our inheritance, we may never live in heaven again!* We can visit it, but once God's throne is forever on earth, what made heaven, heaven will now be permanently on earth. We always talk about living in heaven, and many who have died do. After the rapture, we will spend some time with them enjoying heaven's glory. But then, we move into our eternal abode on the new earth, there to dwell for all eternity. I don't know why I hadn't been taught that long ago! I wanted it made known in this book!)

In chapter 21, we get our introduction to the new earth and a New Jerusalem, our coming eternal home. When 21:1 speaks of heaven passing away, it refers to the first heaven, our atmosphere, and the second heaven, outer space, not the third heaven where God now dwells (See 2 Cor. 12:2). We won't need the sun or moon to light the skies as 21:23 shows: "The city had no need of the sun or of the moon to shine in it, for the glory of God illuminated it, and the Lamb is its light."

Jesus foretold: "**Immediately after the tribulation of those days shall the sun be darkened, and the moon shall not give her light, and…the stars shall fall from heaven…and the powers of the heavens shall be shaken**" (Matt. 24:29 KJV). Not just the heavens, but also our planet earth will one day be destroyed entirely. Peter spoke of this in 2 Peter 3:10 as: "The day of the Lord." (Again, not one 24-hour period, as Peter explained in 3:8: "With the Lord one day is as a thousand years and a thousand years as one day."). That expression, "The Day of the Lord," is used 24 times in the Old Testament to speak of a time of God's judgment on earth, which both Israel and other foreign nations already experienced.

"**But the day of the Lord will come as a thief in the night, in which the heavens will pass away with a great noise, and the elements will melt with fervent heat; both the earth and the works that are in it will be burned up**" (1 Peter 3:10). Did you catch that "thief in the night?" And this certainly is not talking about the rapture! It's the end of the world!

(Again, I am not an environmentalist because God is not! He intends to destroy our whole planet!)

This new earth the Lord will create will be very different from the one where we now live. For one thing, John says of this new earth: "**there was no more sea**" (20:1). I used to be a deep-sea fisherman while pastoring a church for a decade (1985-1995) in Los Angeles County, not far from the ocean. I remember reading this chapter in Revelation and being sad I wouldn't be able to go deep-sea fishing anymore!

Sorry, hunters and fisherman. Since there will be no more death, those sports will have to be replaced with some other activities. But then, maybe hunters will go hunting with some kind of nerf-ball rifle, and animals will joyfully hide behind things and try to outwit hunters.

John says in 20:4: "The former things have passed away." God is so good. How could our coming reward be complete bliss if we just kept thinking about our saddest experiences in life or memories of those who didn't make it to heaven and are now in hell? The Lord (understanding our human tendencies) will take care of any nostalgia or sadness about past events, as Isaiah wrote: **"For behold, I create new heavens and a New Earth; And THE FORMER SHALL NOT BE REMEMBERED OR COME TO MIND"** (Isaiah 65:17).

Don't get too attached to life in this world! John also wrote in 1 John 2:15: **"Love not the world, neither the things that are in this world."** One day soon, we will kiss everything in this world "Goodbye!" (except, thank God, for our loved ones who join us on the new earth!).

On the new earth, God's headquarters will be set up in a newly created Jerusalem: **"I saw...New Jerusalem, coming down out of heaven from God, prepared as a bride adorned for her husband."** (21:2).

There are a few interesting things about this New Jerusalem...

> 1. It has walls: **"It had a great and high wall"** (21:12). If the eternal city of Jerusalem has walls, is it evil for America to have walls bordering our land? This is something to think about.

> 2. Also, the size of this city is amazing: **"The city is laid out as a square, and its length is as great as its breadth...and height"** (21:17). An angel measures it out, and the city is, "twelve thousand furlongs." That computes to approximately 1380 miles wide and 1380 miles high! That is like a gigantic city stretching from Los Angeles to Houston, Texas, and from Los Angeles to the Canadian border! Now that is BIG!

We will probably need a city that big because so many millions of people will live there! (Also, if there is a resurrection of dead pets, and I believe there is, we will need space for the zillions of cats and dogs running around!). Jesus said in John 14:1: "**In my Father's house are many mansions**" (Greek: rooms or dwelling places). This is likely why it is 1380 miles high! It will need to house God's people from 6000 years of history. And, because it is so high, it must be more like a fabulous condominium complex (like Trump Tower in Las Vegas) than a golden street where you see a mansion on the left and one on the right as you walk.

Take another look at 21:4: "**And God will wipe away every tear from their eyes, there shall be no more death, sorrow, or crying; and there shall be no more pain, for the former things have passed away.**"

Some of you may have been crying a lot lately. Think of it, God himself will "wipe away every tear." (Talk about love and intimacy!).

You've shed tears for a dying loved one. Comfort yourself with this truth: "**there shall be no more death.**"

Today, are you sorrowful or depressed? Be encouraged! Soon "**there will be no more sorrow.**"

Maybe you're in a lot of pain. You'll never have that agony ever, ever again because you are promised: "**There shall be no more pain.**"

Anything you're going through, perhaps even as you are reading this, will soon be just one of those "**former things (that) have passed away.**"

Yes, this fallen planet certainly has its disadvantages, but keep in mind always that we will one day dwell on:

The New Earth!

Chapter 22

All Curses Gone!

"And there shall be no more curse" (Rev. 22:6).

The last chapter Revelation, reveals a few more features of the world to come, the promise of Christ's coming, and some warnings. Describing the new earth, John says, **"On either side of the river, was the tree of life…and the leaves of the tree were for the healing of the nations." (22:2).**

We saw in chapter 21 that God makes all things new, and in Isaiah, that the things of the old earth won't even come to our minds again. However, as usual with superlatives in the Bible, there are exceptions, and verse two shows us one of these exceptions. It was the refusal by Adam and Eve to obediently partake of the tree of life only (and not from the tree of the knowledge of good and evil) that caused man's fall and the death, pain, and diseases that followed.

Throughout eternity, we will all have the privilege of eating the fruit of the tree of life, transplanted on the new earth, I think, as a continual reminder that our Lord had to suffer to save us from man's fall because of man's rebelliously partaking of the tree of the knowledge of good and evil.

Then it adds, "**the leaves of the tree were for the healing of the nations.**" Why would we need "healing" when sickness is forever done away with? We won't! These "**leaves**" will serve as an ongoing reminder that on our fallen earth, we were subjected to curses, like sickness and disease, and only Christ's death on the cross redeemed us from such things.

I promise you nobody will ever approach Jesus in eternity and ask Him, *"Lord, I forget; why are those terrible scars in your hands?"* The joy and privilege of eternally praising our Savior will only be fully realized because redeemed mankind will be ever conscious of the fact we were saved from "**so great a death**" (2 Cor. 1:10), and will glory in that fact for an eternity. Those ugly yet beautiful scars on Christ's hands will serve as an ample reminder of our previous lives on the now-destroyed earth.

But there are other reasons we will need at least some reminders of our past life on earth. When 14:11 says of those in hell: "**And the smoke of their torment ascends up forever and ever,**" this "smoke" is not just a graphic description of the ongoing level of the pain of hell but also reveals that those of us enjoying the new earth will be able to view, at times from afar, this smoke which "ascends up forever and ever." And this smoke will thus serve as an eternal reminder of what our Lord saved us from! Like a mother, safely outside with her two little children in her arms, viewing her smoldering house, who turns again and again to thank the fireman who had saved her family, so we also will often turn from the view of that smoking, fiery furnace of hell, to worship Him and thank our Lord once again for His sacrifice which delivered us from that lake of fire.

Rev. 22:3: "**And there shall be no more curse.**" The present earth is cursed! Iniquities, weeds, hard work, painful childbirth, sickness, aging, pain, and death are all results of a curse on earth. Thank God, all these things will soon be forever gone! For now, we're still fighting against them.

Someone dear to me divorced her husband for another man and lived with him for a while before she realized she had made a big mistake. Her new man proved to be very sexually abusive, and she left him within months. Her first husband accepted her and their children back again into his home and paid for her divorce so they could remarry. Unfortunately, though, during that brief affair, she became pregnant with the man's child.

About this time, as I was deeply concerned about her welfare, in the middle of the night, the Lord spoke to me the word, "Tophet." Tophet was a name given to "The Valley of Hinnom." This was an area outside of Jerusalem where backslidden Israelites would sacrifice their children by burning them to death to the heathen God, Molech. Because of this unspeakable act, the area had been desecrated (cursed) and was now useful only as a garbage dump.

So here, in Tophet, the citizens of Jerusalem would dispose of the carcasses of animals that had been used in sacrifices to God. Then, these bodies would be set on fire. Thus, it was a place called "Gehenna," which was the term used by Jesus to describe hell: "**Hell (Gehenna) the fire that never shall be quenched: where their worm dieth not, and the fire is not quenched**" (Mark 9:43, 44 KJV).

In seeking to make Israel understand how awful hell really was, Jesus used this dump to help describe it. Israelites could glance over toward Gehenna and see smoldering carcasses, filled with maggots, and puffs of smoke rising from this cursed place. This picture should send shudders up all our spines as we realize how awful hell must be since this, the worst possible place in Israel, was exactly what the Lord chose to help us visualize the eternal, never-ending horror of hell.

When the Lord spoke "Tophet" to me that night, I felt He was saying this errant wife had put a curse on her children by her adulterous actions (like the Israelites burning their children to death in Tophet). I felt possibly one of her children would die! Because of this revelation, I began to stand in the gap for her and her children.

In my intercessory prayers, I thus began claiming the Galatians 3:13 promise to break this curse (of Tophet) off that family: **"Christ has redeemed us from the curse......having become a curse for us (for it is written, 'Cursed is everyone who hangs on a tree').**" When she gave birth to the child, conceived in her "adulterous" affair, the doctors soon discovered the newborn was absent one gene, which meant it was likely to have physical or mental problems. The child did not die (There is power in prayer!) but did indeed develop physical and mental problems!

When God's Word says, there will be no more curses on the new earth, such curses as that above will be done away with (curses repeated over and over throughout families in this fallen world). Yes, we are all in some measure affected by numerous curses, but Christ's invasion of this planet beginning in a manger and finishing on a cross (where Christ said, "It is finished!") is our assurance of ultimate victory!

Until then, these curses are NOT broken automatically, and we must still contend against them on this side of Christ's return. 22:3 should encourage us. Yes, you are in the heat of the battle because of curses. But soon...*"There shall be no more curse."*

Tell Them "Come!"

"The Spirit and the Bride say 'Come!'" (22:17)

This is the final chapter of the Book of Revelation, wrapping up the closing revelations that John received. Consider the following observations with me…

Those who refuse the mark have this glorious truth to look

forward to: "And they shall see His face. And His name shall be on their foreheads" (22:4). A 666 or His name: everyone in the closing period will have their "mark" for eternity. Have you made your choice yet?

"The Lord...sent His angel to show His servants the things which must shortly take place" (22:6). Since these revelations were given nearly 2,000 years ago, God's idea of "shortly" and ours are very different! But He could be saying that once these things begin to be fulfilled, it will all be concluded in a relatively short period of time. Further evidence for this is in 22:7: "Behold, I am coming quickly!" Since Jesus hasn't come for two millennia, we must assume He meant, *"Once these Revelation events start unfolding, my return will be very soon!"*

Then John is commanded 22:10: "Do not seal the words of the prophecy of this book, for the time is at hand." Or in the GNT: "Do not keep the prophetic words of this book a secret, because the time is near when all this will happen."

I thank God that in His goodness for all these centuries, the book of Revelation has been available for His people to study and read, not as some cryptic unknowable mystery book, but rather one full of important discernible truths of the final approach and landing of Christ's kingdom on this planet. The first time I ever remember reading Revelation was when I was waiting for my mom in our car outside of a laundromat. I was maybe 11 and was in awe of some things I read. God wants everyone, even children, to be in awe and expectation of glorious end time events!

Then 22:11 adds a very sobering truth "He who is unjust, let him be unjust still; he who is filthy, let him be filthy still; and he who is righteous, let him be righteous still; he who is holy, let him be holy still." Here is a description of the eternal state of the dead. Those who are lost will stay lost and, throughout eternity, remain "unjust" and "filthy." The "righteous" and "holy" will eternally stay that way. There is no purgatory. There is no second chance or change in the hearts of both the unsaved and the saved. What a challenge to "be ready," as Christ warned us!

Rev. 22:12: **"My reward is with Me, to give to every one according to his work."** Serve the Lord with all your heart! Do as many good deeds and righteous acts as you can. Your eternal rewards are determined by the accumulation of a Spirit-enabled lifetime of service to Christ.

Rev. 22:14: **"Blessed are those who do His commandments, that they may have the right to the tree of life, and may enter through the gates into the city."** Again, eternal privileges are not just for those who believe but for those who also **"do His commandments."**

Then we see what happens to those who do not keep His commandments: **"But outside** (of the gates of the New Jerusalem City, not nearby but a long distance away in hell!) **are ...sorcerers and sexually immoral and murderers and idolaters"** (22:15).

Then comes our call to evangelism in 22:17: "**And the Spirit and the bride** (that's us!) **say, "Come!"**

The Spirit of God is seeking to draw men and women to Jesus. But He needs our help to do this. Evangelism is how we say, **"Come!"** to the lost and dying. You say "come" to sinners every time you pray for their salvation, every time you witness to them, every time you give them a tract, and every time you invite them to church.

Maybe evangelizing the lost is very difficult for your personality. I have written two books to help you!

EVANGELIST: MY LIFE STORY; MY LIFE JOURNEY

(My autobiography is full of many stories and pictures and shows you how to witness more effectively and win souls.)

ABOUT THE FUTURE (A book written specifically for Christians to give to the unchurched and unsaved. It's only 114 pages. It has 12 excellent, full-page digital pictures and large, easy-to-read print. As of today, it is only $5.55 on Amazon. You can also get it at Barnes & Noble or through your local bookstore. I sell these at near cost when ordered in quantities for churches or serious personal evangelists. Just email me and tell me how many: **evangelist@deawarford.org** or go to my website at www.deawarford.org and hit the link that says Books.)

As the bride of Christ, saying "**Come**" is one of our most important duties. Today, let us all make a fresh commitment to do so! In fact, Jesus is still waiting for His church to fulfill His command in Matthew 24:14: "**This gospel of the kingdom will be preached in all the world as a witness to all the nations, and THEN the end will come.**"

Let us continue to endure whatever we must, and let us join together to get this gospel of the kingdom out to "**all the world**" because...

Christ cannot and will not come until we do!

It All Ends With Grace

"The grace of our Lord Jesus Christ
be with you all. Amen" (22:21).

Jesus began the Book of Revelation in chapter 1:1, and so, fittingly, He ends His book in the last verse, 22:21. But, after all, He is "the Alpha and the Omega, the beginning and the end" (22:13).

When Jesus told John, "**Surely I am coming quickly,**" John responded by saying, "**Come, Lord Jesus!**" John was eager for Christ's return! "To those who eagerly wait for Him, He will appear a second time" (Heb. 9:28). Do you also "eagerly" look forward to His coming? To those in love with the world, the thought of Christ coming is not precious, and they, in fact, dread His coming!

Finally, after 22 chapters of horrific descriptions, scenes of death, misery, and the torments of hell, along with many warnings to not only believe but also to keep His commandments, John wants to encourage us all with a final blessing in 22:21: "**The grace of our Lord Jesus Christ be with you all.**"

"Saved by grace" has been the joyful confession of the redeemed throughout the centuries. Though I work hard to please Him and do righteous acts, I know that He alone deserves all the glory for anything accomplished in my life (like this book in your hands!). I know it is just grace that has kept me all these years. You do, too, don't you? (This would be a perfect time to pause from reading and praise Him for His grace!).

At the very close of this church age, we will have fought a tremendous fight against every attempt by Satan and maybe even the Antichrist to destroy our faith. But then, after we've at last found ourselves safe and rejoicing around Christ's throne, we will cast our crowns at His feet and acknowledge once again and forevermore, "Saved by grace!"

As the author of this book, I can think of no better way to end this teaching on Revelation than to speak the same blessing to you today that John spoke over the church forever...

"The grace of our Lord Jesus Christ be with you all."

"Blessed is he who reads, and those who hear the words of this prophecy, and keep those things which are written in it; for the time is near" (Revelation 1:3).

Evangelist Dea Warford

Email: evangelist@deawarford.org

warford7@hotmail.com

To receive Dea's daily email teachings free, you may sign up and also order the other books he has written at his website:

www.deawarford.org

Made in the USA
Columbia, SC
29 September 2024